Building Countryside Paths and Tracks

Throughout Britain, highly skilled craftspeople work tirelessly in order to maintain the public right of way network.

Building Countryside Paths and Tracks

ANDY RADFORD

THE CROWOOD PRESS

First published in 2006 by
The Crowood Press Ltd
Ramsbury, Marlborough
Wiltshire SN8 2HR

www.crowood.com

British Library Cataloguing-in-Publication Data
A catalogue record for this book is available from the British
Library.

ISBN 1 86126 852 1
EAN 978 1 86126 852 5

Dedication
For Grace and Jenner.

Typeset by Carreg Limited, Ross-on-Wye, Herefordshire

Printed and bound in Great Britain by The Cromwell Press,
Trowbridge

CONTENTS

	Acknowledgements	6
	Introduction	7
1	Getting Started	15
2	Understanding Rights of Way Navigation	30
3	Access for All	41
4	Revetment Boarding	65
5	Natural Stone Revetments	75
6	Gabions	80
7	Building Wooden Steps	84
8	Building Stone Steps and Landings	105
9	Wooden Stiles	116
10	Stone Stiles	119
11	Dealing with Erosion	125
12	Lowland Paths and Bridleways	138
13	Footbridges	155
14	Fingerposts and Way Marks	167
	Useful Organizations	171
	Glossary	173
	Index	175

ACKNOWLEDGEMENTS

I would like to thank the following individuals and organizations for their valuable help with this book:

The Peak District National Park Authority, and members of the Peak Park Countryside Maintenance Team, which includes Pam Pickering, Graham Phillips, Mark Priestley, Andy Bentham and Eleanor Dunn.

Officers of the Peak Park's Ranger Service, including Sean Prendegast, Mike Rhodes, Paul Hopkins, Pete Hardwick, Steve Bell, Tony Hood and David Cramp.

Officers and volunteers of Denbighshire's Countryside Service, including Lucy Bick, Dave Smith, Sam Williams, Allison Phillip and David Shiel.

Members of Countryside Skills, including Kevin Jones, Shane Hughes and Richard Jones.

Members of the Snowdonia Upland path Partnership Project including Alan Hughes, Eilir Parry, Benj Griffiths, Iwan Roberts, Terry Saynor and Sion Jones.

Matt Buckler and Carol Parsons of Moors for the Future Partnership.

INTRODUCTION

In Britain, access through lowland pastures is only made possible via a network of public rights of way, routes where one has a lawful right to walk, ride a horse, or pedal a cycle, depending on the path's designation. The majority of public rights of way bisect private land, and technically you are only allowed to travel the path's designated line to the next access point, be it a gate, stile or other form of countryside furniture. Even stopping for a picnic could, in reality, constitute a trespass, but most landowners tend to turn a blind eye to benign activities such as this, and as long as the walker acts sensibly and within the law, relationships between farmer and visitor usually remain on an even keel.

Who is legally responsible for public rights of way? It is a joint responsibility between the landowner and the Local Highways Authorities. The owner, if a path crosses his or her land, has a duty in law to allow public access at all times, twenty-four hours a day, seven days a week and fifty-two weeks a year. He or she is not allowed to obstruct a public path in any way that will impede a user's right of access; this includes erecting barriers on access points, allowing hedgerows to overgrow in such a way that the branches form an obstruction, or diverting a route without prior planning consent. It does not matter whether the path is in open pasture or follows a route down a farm or house driveway: the same laws apply.

Local Highways Authorities are responsible for the surface of the path and the maintenance on the said surface. They have responsibilities concerning the marking of routes from roads, usually in the form of 'way marks', and keeping accurate documentation of all public rights of way in their jurisdictions. Although local authorities and countryside services sometimes install and maintain stiles and gates, it is really the responsibility of landowners to make sure that adequate access furniture is put in place and maintained. As a path user you have a duty in law to make sure the route is used according to its lawful purpose. For example, you cannot ride a pedal cycle or an equine on a public footpath, but you can on a bridleway.

One of the most important things to establish before any work on a public right of way is commenced is where the definitive line of the path runs. An existing track on the ground is not necessarily the official route, and to insert an access point without first checking its definitive line could lead to problems in the future, not least with an irate landowner. Most public paths cross private land, so any deviation off a designated route is considered an unlawful trespass. If the farmer is affable, hikers can usually get away with this type of misdemeanour; but this would not be the case if you are working for the authority responsible for its maintenance – especially if you have inadvertently inserted a stile on a private track. Any public right of way furniture has to be installed accurately, on the path's correct line; technically it is part of highways law.

Ordnance Survey Maps

All local authorities in the United Kingdom maintain what are called 'definitive maps', documents that actually depict the official public rights of way they are responsible for. The Ordnance Survey produces these maps, usually 1:10,000 scale, for Her Majesty's Stationery Office (HMSO). The cartography is extremely accurate, showing everything but contour lines in one grid square. The Ordnance Survey (OS) have been mapping Britain, producing credible pictures of the ground, since the eighteen-hundreds. The fact that they are so precise means that local authorities can use them to help archive public paths they are accountable for. You can use these maps for accurate footpath surveys and correct positioning of furniture such as gates and stiles (explained later).

Types of Ordnance Survey Map

The Ordnance Survey has produced an array of maps that are available to the public. These are as follows:

1:50,000 Land Ranger series: These maps are fine for route planning and navigating country lanes by motor vehicle. They display most tourist information including public rights of way, but they are not an ideal tool for accurate footpath surveys and practical work.

1:25,000 Explorer: Depicting 2.5in to 1 mile (4cm to 1km). Designed for the walker, the 1:25,000 maps show more detail than the 1:50,000 series, perhaps the most useful being the position of field and garden boundaries. This size of map is the least one should work with when navigating and building paths. Smaller versions of the 1:25,000 series, called Pathfinders, are also available. Pathfinder maps encompass an area of 20 × 20 grid squares and are referenced as such, preceded by their national grid reference prefix (explained in detail later). The Ordnance Survey also supplies 1:25,000 covering just 10 × 10 grid squares. These smaller versions are less cumbersome to open in windy conditions, and are therefore easy to work with when dealing with rights of way in the field.

1:10,000 Definitive maps: These maps are not easily available to the public (although you can purchase them from HMSO). As explained earlier, each map shows everything within a single grid square in 'zoomed-in' detail. They depict major features including buildings, rights of way, field boundaries and rivers, which makes them an ideal reference for the countryside professional. A 1:10,000 is the map that footpath officials consult for research and planning, and for implementing practical tasks.

Map Scales Explained

There is a simple method of explaining what 1:50,000 or 1:25,000 means. If one inserts a pin into a 1:50,000 map, this will be equivalent to 50,000 of the same size pins on the ground: 1pin = 50,000 pins.

Types of Access and their Identification

Public footpaths: The only traffic allowed on this path are walkers or people using invalid carriages, wheelchairs, pushchairs or prams. It is illegal to ride pedal cycles, motor vehicles and ride equines on these routes. Footpaths are shown as small, broken dashes, coloured red on 1:50,000 maps and green on 1:25,000 maps.

Public bridleways: This designation embraces all traffic including pedestrians, pedal cycles, equines, wheelchairs and invalid carriages. It is illegal to drive motor vehicles of any kind. Bridleways are shown as larger, broken dashes, coloured red on 1:50,000 maps and green on 1:25,000 maps.

Byway or green lane: Before the amendments introduced by the Country-side and Rights of Way Act 2000 (ex-plained later), a byway was open to all vehicular traffic. Since the act, the use of byways is now limited to the same traffic described for bridleways. Byways are shown as red crosses on 1:50,000 maps and green crosses on 1:25,000 maps.

Byway Open to All Traffic (BOAT): A route open to all traffic, but local authorities can impose restrictions.

Road Used as Public Path (RUPP): The Countryside and Rights of Way Act 2000 (explained later) has changed the designation of these paths, and they have now been reclassified as 'restricted byways'; this now means that motor vehicles can no longer be driven along these routes. Before reclassification a RUPP was open to all traffic.

Other routes with public access are shown as red dots on the 1:50,000 maps and green dots on the 1:25,000 maps.

National trails/long-distance routes: Since the designation of the Pennine Way, Britain's first long-distance footpath, many national trails have followed in its wake. National trails are shown as red diamonds on the 1:50,000 maps and green diamonds on the 1:25,000 maps. These routes, from start to finish, can include public footpaths, bridleways, BOATs and even some 'permitted routes'.

A permitted route is not a public right of way, it is a track where the landowner has given permission for access, usually by agreement with a local authority. In some cases a landowner will allow the use of land for hobbies such as 'off-roading' or for equines. The fact that users do not have a legal right to use permitted paths means that access can be closed at any time the owner sees fit.

In recent years, due to the popularity of off-road cycling, a new style of privately agreed route has come into existence: off-road cycle routes.

Routes depicted with black dashes or dots are private roads or tracks. As such, the public does not have permission to enter the land unless the landowner grants permission or they cross upland areas and commons that fall within the scope of the Countryside and Rights of Way Act 2000.

The History of Access

Britain has a vast web of public rights of way, a tradition that sets us apart from most countries. No matter where you travel in the United Kingdom, you are not far from an area where the public has the right of access. Many routes, especially the oldest, will have an interesting history; even the little-used byway snaking down from an uninhabited hillside, seemingly terminating nowhere in particular, can generally tell a story of a bygone age. Most people are aware of the historical significance of straight Roman roads, but why do some rural footpaths, after traversing miles of countryside, end in a church or chapel graveyard, and not an interconnecting village? What is the point of the road that begins in one town, scales the high point of a desolate moorland, then winds its way to the town on the other side?

The graveyard path would have had the morbid title 'Dead Man's Way', and described the road along which the residents of an outlying village would carry the coffins of dead relatives to be buried in the ground. The road across the moor would probably have been an old drovers' route, a highway where traders carried their goods to neighbouring markets.

Sometimes the name of a path gives away its historical purpose; Salters' Way or Salters' Lane, for example, tells us that the route was once used to transport salt. Cheshire and Staffordshire have many salters' lanes due to their underground salt mines. Road names prefixed with the word 'Lud' are commonly found near places with a lead-mining tradition, 'lud' being the Roman word for 'lead'.

The majority of today's public paths began as workers' access routes, or as a shortcut to the local alehouse, church or store: they all served a specific, practical purpose other than just going for a leisurely stroll. These thoroughfares were not rights of way, since the gentry who owned the land owned them, too. In fact the favourite route you walk on today was more than likely conceived before the notion of 'public path' entered the British way of life.

The British countryside is one of the most diverse landscapes in the world. The lazy idyll of lowland, its fertile pastures bisected by hedgerows, brooks and secluded lanes, soon changes to highland outcrops of rugged terrain, typified by moorland wilderness and windswept precipices. With the exception of small pockets of land, this rural vista is privately owned, accessed only by public rights of way or negotiated access agreements. Until recently the public has only been able to walk over private moorland and downland by virtue of access agreements negotiated between landowners and local authorities. Thus the public did not have an automatic right to use this land: this was entirely dependent on the good will of the individual farmer, an arrangement based on trust between walker, local authority and the farming community.

Rights of Access and Legislative Change

The new Countryside and Rights of Way Act 2000 (the CRoW Act 2000) was inaugurated in the Peak Park in September 2004. The CRoW Act represents one of the most significant changes to the rural environment for many years, and will enhance the manner in which the public can utilize the benefits of open country.

These new rights of access to open country are rooted in a century's worth of campaigns and various legislative changes. In 1725 journalist and writer Daniel Defoe described Derbyshire's High Peak as 'The most desolate, wild, abandoned country in Britain'; and William Wordsworth's prose, describing the dreamy beauty of his much-beloved Lake District, is a national treasure. In 1865 the Common, Open Spaces and Footpath Preservation Society was formed to save Epping Forest, Wimbledon Common and Hampstead Heath. The genesis of the 'right to roam' idea began in 1876 with the creation of the Hayfield and Kinder Scout Ancient Footpaths Association.

Interest in rambling grew during Queen Victoria's reign, but an 'Access to Mountains' bill failed to make it through parliament in 1884. In 1894, though, an amendment to the Local Government Act was added to allow a proviso for some public rights of way. In 1895 the National Trust was formed with a remit to preserve places of historic interest and areas of natural beauty. In 1908 a second attempt to push through the Access to Mountains Bill collapsed, and a third attempt failed in 1926; but by this time there were more organizations and societies dedicated to nature conservation and woodland protection, and the Law of

Property Act 1925 yielded one of the first rights of access to all urban commons in England and Wales.

In 1927 and 1932 two significant events in rambling history occurred. The first was a mass trespass organized by a Sheffield rambling club, which took place at Derbyshire's Winnat's Pass. The second – perhaps the most famous of all protests – was the mass trespass on Kinder Scout, where 400 ramblers came into conflict with gamekeepers and landowners, resulting in a number of arrests. The ramblers then declared a victory when the Rights of Way Act was passed. At the end of the 1920s and through the next decade, the concept of Britain's national parks was set into motion, inspired by Yellowstone in the USA, the world's first national park set up in 1872. By 1939, after three failed attempts, the Access to Mountains Act eventually made it through parliament.

Britain had now accepted that there was a demand to enjoy the pleasures of open country, and in 1942 the Scott Report concluded there was a need for national parks. This was followed by the Dower Report of 1945, a study into how national parks would work in England and Wales.

During the next six years the rural environment underwent important changes in legislation: in 1947 the Town and Country Planning Act, setting up a land-use planning system, and in 1949 the National Parks and Access to the Countryside Act, became enshrined into the British way of life. The latter act also brought about the Countryside Commission (now called the Countryside Agency), the Nature Conservancy Council (now named English Nature), and the provision for ten national parks. The act also provided for 'Areas of Outstanding Natural Beauty' (AONBs).

On 17 April 1951 the Peak District was established as Britain's first national park; it delivered the first access agreements, whereby people were allowed to walk over private moorland. That same year Snowdonia, the Lake District and Dartmoor were given national park status.

In 1957 a further six national parks were designated: the Pembrokeshire coast, the North York moors, the Yorkshire Dales, Exmoor, Northumberland and the Brecon Beacons. By 1968 the government had passed the Countryside Act, followed by the Wildlife and Countryside Act in 1981 and the Rights of Way Act in 1991. The Environment Act of 1995 established the Environment Agency, the coming together of two statutory bodies, her Majesty's Inspectorate of Pollution (HMIP) and the National Rivers Authority (NRA).

The Countryside and Rights of Way Act 2000

Britain's latest environment legislation is the Countryside and Rights of Way Act 2000. CRoW 2000 has given rise to new rights of access on hitherto private and concessionary open country. Whilst beneficial to country lovers, the landowning population treated its inception with trepidation, a fear of a continuing 'right to roam' on to pasture, meadow and arable farmland. Needless to say, the act does not allow blanket access to every enclosure, only those on moorland, down, heath, uplands and common. CRoW 2000 also saw the production of a new Country Code, which explains visitor and landowner rights and responsibilities.

The act also pays attention to the setting up of 'access forums'. There are two types of access forum: a national forum chaired by the deputy chair of the Countryside Agency, and local access forums consisting of interested user groups within a local or national park authority. The national forum was primarily developed to balance the interests of major landowning bodies and rights of way user groups. Organizations represented include the National Farmers Union, the British Horse Society, the Country Land and Business Association, the Ramblers Association and the National Trust, to name but a few. Local access forums consist of landowners, representatives of local rights of way user groups and other interested bodies. Their role is to advise the local authority on access issues and rights of way improvement plans.

This act is made up of five parts. Part 1 concerns access to open country. Part 2 deals with the new variations in the manner in which public rights of way are recorded, including the management and enforcement of public routes. Part 3 is about nature conservation and the protection of wildlife. Part 4 strengthens the statutory basis of Areas of Outstanding Natural Beauty (AONBs). Part 5 pays attention to the setting up of access forums. There isn't room here to discuss all five parts of the act, only the most interesting ones, Parts 1 to 3. The act can be viewed in full on the Countryside Agency's website, listed at the back of this book.

Under Part 1 of the act the public has rights to designated 'access land' for open-air recreation on foot. Horse riding and cycling are not permitted unless there is an existing public bridleway, or the landowner has dedicated an area for this purpose. Other activities excluded from the act include driving a vehicle (excluding an invalid carriage), organized games, the use of a metal detector, taking anything from the land (stones, wood or flora), and lighting or causing fires. The public does not have a right to intentionally disturb livestock, habitats or wildlife.

CRoW includes provision for dog walking, but between 1 March and 31 July animals should be restrained by a leash of no more than 2 metres. The reason for this is to protect livestock and ground-nesting birds during the breeding season. At times there will be restrictions enforced on open country for reasons of public safety, nature conservation and land management.

Part 2 of the act encompasses rights of way and common land, and has created a new category of highway. 'Roads used as public paths' (RUPPs) have been reclassified as 'restricted byways', which now means that motor vehicles can no longer be driven along these routes; before reclassification a RUPP was open to all traffic. Part 2 also gives power to the Countryside Agency for the creation of new public rights of way on land that does not permit access under the new rules. This is a 'reserved power', and it will be the responsibility of the local authorities under the Highways Act 1980 to create rights of way by agreement or order.

Part 2 has added a further section to Section 137 (concerning wilfully obstructing a highway) of the Highways Act 1980. Section 137ZA now empowers magistrates to impose fines of £5,000 on people who fail to comply with orders to remove obstructions. Additional fines can be imposed for each day the offence continues.

Under Section 22 of the Road Traffic Act 1984, local authorities can make 'traffic regulation orders' to help conserve and enhance the natural beauty of an area for public enjoyment. Section 66 of the CRoW Act extends Section 22 to include Sites of Special Scientific Interest (SSSIs). There is also a new section (Section 22A) that enables the control of vehicular traffic on byways and unclassified roads, again for the purpose of conservation and enhancement.

Part 3 of the CRoW Act outlines nature conservation and wildlife protection. This includes a strengthening of the provisions laid down in the Wildlife and Countryside Act 1981 pertaining to some wildlife species, giving police authorities stronger search and seizure powers, including powers of entry to acquire wildlife tissue samples for DNA analysis. It also empowers courts to impose custodial sentences for most offences outlined in Part 1 of the Wildlife and Countryside Act 1981.

The practical groundwork has also been extensive, with a large quantity of gates, stiles and new access signs added to locations that were previously fenced off. The Peak District National Park Authority, for example, has provided considerable resources towards implementing the act within its boundaries. Park officers have liaised with landowners, and extra staff, including an access officer, have been appointed. The Ranger Service, along with a further 100 part-timers (the service already employed 180), patrols the new access areas, advising visitors on their rights and responsibilities under the act.

In Wales the new access rights came into force in April 2005. The Denbighshire Countryside Service, to name but one, with funding from the Countryside Council for Wales (CCW), has devoted many hours to explaining the act, going into schools, making information easily available to the public, and negotiating with landowners. The act, like most new legislation, did not meet with approval from all quarters, and worries about damage and unregulated trespass on to private land were voiced. But at the end of the day, it is not the act that will cause these problems, it is more to do with people's misinterpretations of the law. Furthermore, a vandal will still cause damage, and some people will persist in transgressing on to private land regardless of legislation, either by accident or malicious intent. Most users of open country respect the land and love nature, and as the Peak Park's access agreements of old have shown, visitor and farmer *can* find a successful balance of interests.

CHAPTER 1

GETTING STARTED

Safety

Working in hazardous conditions or in public places, such as on countryside public rights of way, requires a 'risk assessment' by law. By conducting a risk assessment potential hazards can be identified, reduced or even eliminated. Because footpath workers install items that people will use over and over again, and because they will be working in close proximity to members of the public, the reduction and elimination of potential dangers is of vital importance.

A risk assessment is a scrupulous analysis of a future project that weighs up the risks to human welfare from every possible angle. The conclusions of an assessment should tell you if the workforce is able to cope safely, or if they need further training. Unlike a factory workplace where the risks are similar every day, hazards in the open countryside can differ from day to day. The conditions surrounding an upland path project, for example, can shift with every rolling cloud, sometimes more than once in a day. So, how safe is an upland work site, and can it be made safer? Perched on the side of a mountain, is a group of people able to work comfortably without danger to themselves, and are they able to operate safely? Are they able to deal with danger if it should arise? What would happen if a loose boulder fell down the hillside, for example?

The risks will be different for all projects, but one factor remains the same: as project manager, you are liable for anything built on a public path, and this includes bad workmanship and defective materials. Investigators analysing a serious work-related incident will look at the risk assessment to see if the issues leading up to the accident were addressed beforehand. In today's climate of endless litigation, a risk assessment is crucial, especially for the health and well-being of the general public.

It is difficult to quantify the dangers in a book, as no two work areas are alike. One obvious factor, though, is the skill, knowledge and physical health of a work team, who should be able to meet the requirements of every task laid in front of them. Countryside teams are not just highly skilled and fit craftspeople, they are also trained to be aware of their environment and to deal with out-of-the-ordinary events when they happen. Although a site supervisor is responsible for health and safety, everyone should hold a first-aid certificate, and know how to deal with a casualty before help arrives, which could be some time. In the event of an injured climber or hiker, there is every possibility that a countryside team will be the first to attend the casualty, simply because they are already working close by; and there might also be the unforeseen prospect of a colleague falling ill.

The skills required to look after a casualty at over 2,000ft (600m) are very different from those demanded in factory-floor first aid. Paramedics arrive quickly in towns, and it isn't long before a casualty is in skilful hands; but trained mountain rescue teams take much longer to appear. They have to be called in from their place of work, gathered together, briefed and kitted up before they even start their ascent of the hill. Mind you, if a risk assessment threw up this scenario, you would probably put the proposed project on 'hold', and get on with some cosy number by the side of a river. But then you would have to deal with the possibility of someone falling in – and that's the very nature of what can happen in countryside work.

An inspection of a future work site will reveal the obvious hazards, and a reassessment of the findings will bring the less obvious to light. A site meeting with the work team may point out things that were not initially evident, and it will give the team members a chance to personally attune themselves with the job in relation to their own safety.

A completed risk assessment will have recognized the major and minor hazards, identified the ability of the team and decided if further training is required. The assessment should have noted how far from civilization the task will be taking place, including all possible escape routes off a mountain if things should go wrong, and it should describe how long it would take qualified medical help to arrive. The nature of the work and the task itself will dictate the number of operatives necessary for the safe completion of the project, and some form of communication such as a two-way radio or mobile phone is vital when working in mountainous regions.

Safety in the Working Countryside

No matter what industry you work in, health and safety at work is a lawful requirement. Every working practice has a safe method, and every tool comes with a recommended technique of operation. The government's Health and Safety Executive (HSE) oversees safety in the workplace, and can exercise powers of criminal prosecution over employers and employees who breach health and safety law. In most cases the defendant is fined a substantial sum of money (usually employers), however the more serious incidents can lead to a custodial sentence.

The onus is on the employer to make sure adequate training is given, but the employee has a duty to translate that training into safe working practices. Serious breaches of health safety law made by an employee will more than likely lead to his/her instant dismissal. The Health and Safety at Work Law exists to protect the worker, the management team and the general public, and is built on years of knowledge and experience gained from past industrial accidents.

As with any industrial working environment where the use of heavy tools and machinery is commonplace, safety has to be the first consideration. There are many dangers associated with working on practical tasks in the open countryside, especially when terrain, weather conditions and tools are taken into account at the same time. The aim of this book is not to teach HSE law, but I feel it is important to discuss the basic, safe operation of the tools needed to perform common countryside tasks.

Operative Tools

Fencing Tools

A **universal fencing tool** (or fencing pliers) is a multi-purpose tool incorporating a wire strainer, wire cutter, hammer, staple gouge and staple-pulling jaw. The main injuries and problems associated with these tools include, first, bruised fingers due to cutting wire when the tool is blunt or the wire is very high tensile: very painful, and occurs because too much force has to be used. Once the cutter severs the wire, the 'grip' pressure turns to inertia. Other injuries include gashes and piercing. It is good practice not to use fencing pliers for tensioning long or continuous sections of barbed wire because the hand must be held so close to the barbs.

Fencing strainers (sometimes called chain-strainers or monkey strainers) are a specialist tool, designed for applying high tension to stock netting and wire. Over-straining will snap the wire, causing it to coil back towards the direction of tension. Injuries associated with this tool are broken and bruised knuckles and fingers, including deep wounds due to coiled-back wire. This is one reason why chain-strainers should not be used for straining barbed wire.

The ideal tool for this purpose is called a 'bar strainer'; it has a wire grip and a long torsion handle, and is ideal for applying light to medium tension on wire

– in some cases, it's the only straining tool you'll need. For tensioning barbed wire, the bar strainer comes into its own. Barbed wire at the best of times is awkward to work with, and when over-tensioned can brook disaster. A bar strainer relies solely on the fencer's own strength to pull the wire, therefore reducing the risk of breakage and of coil-back. This tool is useful for straining short sections of fence line of up to 16.5ft (5m); stretches of wire longer than this will require heavy-duty chain strainers.

Long-Handled and Large Tools

These include sledge hammers, fencing mauls, picks, mattocks, tampers (also called 'punners'), spades, shovels and crowbars. Of all non-mechanical work tools, it is this category that has the potential to cause severe harm. The implements that are swung in 'arc' fashion include sledge hammers, picks, mattocks and mauls, and these pose the most serious threat to colleagues and members of the public. Working safely with these tools is a fusion of skill, strength, balance, grip, accuracy and spatial awareness. Because they are top heavy they must be correctly applied at all times; on no account should they be swung above head height, as this could result in a loss of control and grip. Used properly, the body will compensate for the tool's lack of balance by bending forwards with the downward swing. The human back, however, is inflexible and cannot transfer energy if used incorrectly; thus a mattock swung backwards above head height may cause the user to fall over, possibly on the tool, or the tool to fly backwards through the air.

Grip is equally important. All tool shafts (or stales) rely on friction between hands and handle, and most work gloves will not afford the correct amount of friction required for a 'firm grip'. It is therefore recommended that where possible, gloves should not be worn. Adequate warning before operation should also be given, and it is the responsibility of the tool user to ensure that people remain out of harm's way. Injuries associated with the latter include a broken or impaled lower leg due to an incorrect stance, and serious injury to passers-by, mainly through lack of awareness and swinging the tool too high.

A **post slammer** is a hollow metal tube with a handle welded on each side, and is the best manual post-driving tool available. By placing the tube over the top of a fencing stake the operator, holding the handles and using a series of downward thrusts, can easily drive it firmly into the ground. Compared to a fencing maul, the post slammer greatly reduces the time and effort it takes to knock in a line of stakes. When using this tool, protective headwear should be worn at all times.

Spades, shovels, tampers and crowbars are either vertical thrust tools, or are used by force at an angle. However, unless you are totally foolish, the associated risk is mainly to the operator; injuries might include severed and impaled toes, and broken feet. Another hazard associated with spades and crowbars when digging postholes, is hidden power lines. It has been known for workers to inadvertently cut through high voltage cables – the risks involved needing no description. A device called a 'cat scan' will detect any power lines that may be running under the excavation area.

Tools left unattended are another potential cause of harm. A work site should always have a 'safe area', away from the route of a public path. Tools should be stored lying down with the prongs of rakes and forks embedded into the ground. A tool left standing is difficult to see, especially in dim light.

Petrol-Powered Hand Tools

The tools used on a regular basis during countryside work are chainsaws and

Crowbars and spades can penetrate hidden power lines.

brush cutters. In an industrial working environment it is against health and safety regulations to operate any of these without a recognized handler's certificate.

The Chainsaw

Unlike electric bench saws that come with safety guards and emergency cut-off switches, the chainsaw's only safety feature is the chain brake, designed to stop the chain when the saw is propelled into a motion called 'kickback'. This occurs when the tip of the saw's bar (the part of the saw that holds the chain) glances an obstruction, pushing it towards the user's body. The chain brake is designed to hit the back of the hand, instantly stopping the cutting action of the saw. As this device was only added to counter the effects of kickback, the common injuries associated with chainsaws nowadays are mainly to the lower parts of the body, either caused by chain run-on (an action associated with loose and poorly maintained chains, which occurs when the throttle is released and the chain continues to revolve), misuse or user fatigue.

Safety experts soon realized that the only safety device that could be added without hindering the operation of the saw was the chain brake, and so turned their attention towards the user. They came up with the idea of body armour in the form of ballistic nylon clothing, a fabric first used in bullet-proof garments, its composition such that it will clog and stop a chain instantly.

Other essential safety clothing includes purpose-made gloves, footwear, and helmets complete with visors and earmuffs.

The Brush Cutter

A brush cutter is an industrial strimmer with a steel blade attached instead of nylon twine. Although the cutting zone is partially enclosed by a guard, this only offers protection to the operator's body from flying stones and similar projectiles. The blade revolves at very high speeds and is designed for trimming large, woody stems and small tree whips. Nylon twine is intended for cutting grassy growth, but it will still cause small rubble or sticks to spin away if it hits them. As

By using a device called a 'cat scan' you can detect any power cables that may be trailing under your work site.

with a chainsaw, if you use a brush cutter it is mandatory to hold a recognized handling certificate.

Industrial brush cutters or strimmers are heavy, cumbersome tools and should be supported by a dedicated body harness. Eye and ear protection should be worn at all times during operation, as should gloves that help compensate for mechanical vibration.

Heavy and Light Plant Machinery

Some aspects of countryside work involve the use of heavy plant, such as mini diggers and dumpers. No one should be allowed to operate one of these vehicles without first gaining a recognized certificate of competence.

It goes without saying that any work site is a potentially dangerous arena. In the building trade, all sites are separated from the public by high safety fencing, but this is often not possible or practicable in a countryside location because of its very nature. This calls for greater awareness, and diligent adherence to safety policy. When plant is being operated in conditions like this, or in a confined space, the driver must have someone as a lookout.

Plant equipment should never be used for work it is not designed to carry out, and the operator must always be aware of hidden dangers, including underground cables and pipework.

Any warning signs on the vehicle must remain clear and visible; this is especially important on earth-moving equipment that pivots during operation. If the excavator is loading soil or aggregates into another vehicle such as a dumper, the operator of the excavator should ensure that the dumper driver has stopped the engine, dismounted, and is clear of the excavator's swinging arm.

Anybody working in close proximity to heavy plant equipment must always wear ear and head protection.

Small stand-alone concrete mixers should be placed on a level, firm surface, and the loading of sand, cement and aggregates must always be carried out from the side of the bucket, and not from in front, to avoid the likelihood of the shovel catching the internal mixing blades. Cement is an irritant and can affect the skin, eyes, nose and throat, so adequate protection should be worn at all times.

Electrical Power Tools

In the industrial working environment all electrical tools must run on 110 volts, not the UK domestic 240 volts. Any 240-volt tool should be connected to a 110-volt transformer via heavy-duty 110-volt plugs and sockets. Electrical power tools make light work of heavy jobs, and some of the projects described later rely on their use.

As most of the projects in this book are performed in the open countryside, it is essential to abide by the safety advice relating to each item. Very often this comes down to common-sense work practices, such as never using a power tool in wet conditions, always using a circuit breaker, uncoiling extension cables to their full extent, and making sure that they, too, have an integrated circuit breaker. Electrocution is a serious and potentially fatal injury, and all precautions must be taken against it happening. Check the cables of all power tools for splits on the outer insulating sheaths; needless to say, if the cables are worn, the tool should not be used.

Small Hand Tools

Small hand tools pose the greatest threat as far as injury to the user is concerned, for the simple reason that they are used on a regular basis, and close to the body. It is for this reason I have included information regarding their safe use.

- Use the right tool for the right job: improper substitutes may increase the risk of injury, or damage the item under construction.
- Keep tools serviced and in good condition at all times. Wipe metal parts with a rag doused in clean mineral oil after use.
- Always check the tool for defects before use, and replace damaged items.
- All cutting tools should be kept sharp, and when not in use, place suitable covers over blades and saw teeth.
- Mallet shafts and hammer handles should sit tightly within the tool's head.
- Place sharp tools (chisels, saws, marking blades) in the centre of a workbench, making sure blades or handles do not extend off the edge of the bench.
- Store tools in the proper manner after use.
- Wear appropriate safety clothing in relation to the tool in use: for example, goggles and face masks for drills and electric saws.
- The working area must be kept clear of clutter and debris at all times. If the task in hand produces a high quantity of waste, you should clean and sweep it regularly.

- If your work area is small and you are using many tools at the same time, it is a good idea to wear a tool belt to store equipment. This will save space and ensure the working area is clear from obstruction.
- Do not use tools for a job they are not intended to do. For example, refrain from using chisels for levering and wooden mallets for driving in nails and bolts.
- Do not use excessive force on tools that are not designed to take strain.
- Do not transport sharp tools in pockets other than ones designed for them.

Chisels

There are many styles of wood chisel, each one designed for a specific cutting purpose. Use the correct chisel for the job in hand to avoid inaccurate work.

- Wear safety goggles or glasses.
- Ensure that wooden-handled tools are free from cracks, splinters and oily substances.
- Keep the tool sharp at all times by 'honing' the cutting area to the correct angle. Blunt tools will make the work difficult, which could result in an untidy, misaligned joint.
- Make sure there are no foreign bodies in the timber such as screws or nails, as these will blunt or damage the blade.
- When cutting joins or mortises maintain a balanced stance, so if the chisel slips you won't fall over.
- Always make sure that your hands and body are placed behind the cutting edge, and chip timber away from you.
- Do not strike wood chisels with a metal hammer; always use a wooden or rubber mallet with a wide striking surface.

- When finishing a join or mortise, use only hand pressure to smooth away uneven cuts or burrs.
- Always store chisels with their protective cap over the cutting edge.

Hand Saws

Use the right saw for the job. A hacksaw, for example, is used for cutting metal. Check timber for foreign bodies such as nails and screws.

If hand saws are not used correctly, the resulting injury could be severe: considering the pressure used when trimming timber, a slip will easily rip bare flesh to the bone. Always keep to the correct method of operation, which is as follows: begin your cut by placing a hand at the side of the pencil guide, making sure that your thumb is pressed against the side of the metal blade. Start the cut with a slow, careful action to prevent the blade from bouncing on the wood. Only apply pressure on the 'downward' stroke; this will ensure that the actual cutting action is maintained away from the body. Clamp the timber firmly to prevent it from moving.

Replace damaged or severely blunt saws, and keep the saw teeth properly 'set'. Many saws come with a protective plastic cover that fits over the teeth, to protect the tool when stored and reduce the risk of injury.

After each use, wipe the blade (not the handle or grip) with a rag doused in clean mineral oil.

Hacksaws: These saws are designed for cutting metal. The blade should be attached with the teeth pointing forwards.

Use the entire length of the blade when trimming material, working with steady, firm strokes directed away from the body. The backward stroke should be light to eliminate premature blunting of the teeth.

On long jobs the blade and the material will heat up. Avoid touching these with your hand. To prevent the blade from overheating and snapping, light oil can be applied over the cutting area.

Screwdrivers

Choose the correct screwdriver for the style and size of screw – Philips-head drivers for Philips-head screws, Pozidriv for Pozi-head screws.

Pre-drill the pilot holes before joining two sections of timber together to assist the travel of the screw. This is the safest method, as less pressure is applied to the screwdriver; screws will follow the drilled pilot holes instead of going in at an angle, and this also protects the wood from splitting. Make sure that the drilled hole has a smaller diameter than the screw.

Ensure the screwdriver handle is clean and free from grease and oil; an unexpected 'slip' may result in injury and damaged work.

Using a ratchet drive (or Yankee screwdriver) for continuous screw work is healthier for the wrists and results in less fatigue. Other alternatives are powered drivers, or tools with a pistol grip.

Defective screwdrivers – ones with bent shafts, or blunt or broken tips – will continually slip off the screw head, damaging work or causing injury. Wooden handles, if split, should be replaced.

Only use a screwdriver for the job it is intended for. These tools are not pribars, levers or chisels.

Exposing a screwdriver to excessive heat can weaken the metal.

Clamps

Clamps are used for a wide variety of applications; they are very versatile, and hold work securely when you are sawing or chiselling. There are many styles and sizes of this tool available, so it is essential to choose the right one for your work-holding requirements. The main points to consider are the size of timber compared to the opening (or 'reach') of the clamp, and the depth of the clamp's 'throat' in relation to the width of the workload. Trying to secure work in a tool that is too small to handle the weight will result in the timber becoming dislodged. At the opposite end of the spectrum, avoid using an extra large, heavy clamp just because it has a large throat; it is far better to employ a smaller, deep-throated item intended for the size and shape of the timber.

Ensure that the threaded end can turn easily before use. An application of light oil will free moveable parts, but avoid contaminating the 'anvil' and 'pressure plate' sections otherwise it may trickle on to the wood.

Ensure that the pressure plate and anvil come into contact with the work part before tightening. To avoid damage, use a thin wooden 'pad' between the anvil and timber.

Do not use torque bars, hammers or wrenches to tighten clamps; most are only designed for hand tension.

Tools for Cutting Vegetation

Tools in this category are scythes, sickles, brushing hooks, billhooks, axes, bowsaws and loppers. These are perhaps the most dangerous of all small hand tools, and extreme caution must be exercised when working with them. With the exception of loppers and bowsaws, they are used in a downward or swinging arc fashion. A blade when swung with human force can be fatal or at the least cause severe injury.

With any cutting tool a correct, comfortable stance is required, with the angle of the cut taking it away from the body. At the point when the tool cuts vegetation, the blade should be as close to the ground as possible.

Fatigue, lack of concentration and poorly maintained blades and shafts are the major cause of accidents associated with these tools. Bowsaws are more dangerous at the beginning of a cut, as the blade's teeth can 'jump' or bounce on the wood. Loppers are able to sever small tree branches, and will do the same to a finger.

Care must be taken not to cut through wood that is beyond the strength of the tool.

Head and eye protection must be worn at all times.

Leptospyrosis (Weil's Disease)

Incidences of Weil's disease have been increasingly reported in people who work in the countryside; at particular risk are those working in ponds and old drainage gullies. The disease is carried by rats and spread through their urine, and humans can contract it through open wounds and abrasions whilst working in contaminated water. The first signs of infection are influenza-like symptoms. If this occurs soon after a drainage or pond-clearance task, you should consult a doctor immediately. If a blood test confirms the illness, quick treatment is required.

Working with Helicopters

The use of helicopters for airlifting heavy materials to inaccessible works is now very common, and it is normally the work team's responsibility to guide the aircraft in before tools and materials are dropped off. The following notes are an extract from the paper called the 'Pennine Way Management Project Review 1991–2001', written by Mike Rhodes, Peak District National Park Authority, who has kindly given his permission for its reproduction here.

The following account aims to give practical information for the best and safe use of helicopters for load lifting – that is, airlifting materials and equipment to remote locations for footpath works, fencing, revegetation and so on.

The Advantages and Disadvantages of Helicopter Use

Advantages:

* Helicopters are able to move large amounts of material quickly to remote sites.
* Minimal manual handling.
* Helicopters improve on alternative mechanical means such as ATVs (supercats, argocats and quads) by

A helicopter delivers path materials to a Peak District National Park Authority work team (reproduced with permission from Mike Rhodes).

getting materials loaded and dropped where required without any manual handling.

- Materials can be delivered to sites that would be physically impossible to reach by any other means.
- There is no ground damage.
- ATVs carrying large amounts of materials will damage sensitive terrain.

Disadvantages:

- High initial cost. Although helicopters will save money in the long term on labour costs, plant and haulage hire and ground repairs, the high initial cost may be restrictive.
- Gaining permissions to fly from the chosen lift site and over sensitive sites requires considerable advance planning. Stacking, sorting and weighing materials and safety considerations also require careful organization.

The manager responsible for the airlift must ensure the contractor has the experience and capability to carry out the task required, and has appropriate certification

Snowdonia National Park Authority work-team members guide a helicopter for drop-off (reproduced with permission from Snowdonia Upland Path Partnership Project Officer).

and insurance. Commercial companies have a maximum payload of either 1,000kg or 600kg, depending on the machine used, and this can determine the choice of contractor. Payloads larger than this, up to 8,000kg, will require specialist military aircraft such as an RAF Chinook.

Planning an Airlift

The hire and use of helicopters is a relatively straightforward operation. However, a number of logistical questions must be addressed if an airlift is to progress smoothly and with minimum stress and cost. Liaison with the helicopter company is important, as they will need to know:

- What material is to be moved, and how it is to be secured.
- Where the lift site is, and where materials are to be dropped; both need to be plotted on a suitable scale map, with information such as the lateral distance and the height climbed (*see* below for choice of lift site).
- Where there is road access for the groundcrew.
- Locations for a fuel store and refuelling site.
- That all loads conform to the weight limit.
- Overnight accommodation for crew and machine.

At the same time the project manager must ensure that:

- A fixed price contract is drawn up. Prices range from £500 to £700 an hour, although it is best to obtain quotes per load or fixed quantity.

- Quantities needed are accurately calculated.
- Loads are secure and safe before the helicopter arrives.
- Advance warning signs are positioned on roads and footpaths.
- The operation has been carefully planned; this eliminates avoidable delays.
- Sufficient competent staff are available to cover all eventualities; that they have appropriate equipment and are fully briefed.
- All parties that are likely to be affected are informed, for example landowners, tenants, residents, gamekeepers, English Nature.
- Police are informed if necessary (for example in the case of road closures, crowd control).

Choice of Site for Load Lifting

Careful consideration should be given to the choice of lift site. Ideally it should be away from built up areas, and comfortably large enough to allow materials to be stacked evenly, with space for the groundcrew to move about freely.

It should have space for an emergency landing area and refuelling point (these two areas must be well apart and kept clear), and should be uncluttered by trees, masts, pylons or overhead power lines.

It should be clear of rubbish and light debris that could be blown into the air by down-draught (or these should be weighted down), and should have good road access for delivery of materials to the site.

Preparation

To ensure that an airlift goes smoothly and that the best value for money is gained, all loads should be weighed and bundled or bagged prior to the date of the lift. Again, forward planning is essential, and consultation with the helicopter company is strongly recommended.

Regarding the amount of materials moved, different pilots fly different loads at different speeds, but a rule of thumb is that in optimum flying conditions (a smooth airflow of around 20mph (30km) with visibility of 3,000ft (1km) or more), thirty to forty dense loads (for example, stone) per hour may be lifted to a site 1km away with a height rise of less than 150m (500ft) – that is, a 90sec turnaround.

Sling Equipment

Most commercial companies supply their own slings, buckets, skips and so on. Other slings may be used provided they are marked with a 'safe working load' (SWL) and approved by the pilot. A safe working load of twice the suspended load is the usual approved strength for slings.

Personnel

The helicopter company will provide all hooking-on gear and ground staff. The ground staff refuel the aircraft and usually hook on loads. At busy times the project's own staff may be asked to help with hooking on. Staff are usually flown to the drop site prior to the first load, and will be required to indicate the exact site for dropping the loads.

Correct safety clothing is essential.

Safety

Working with helicopters is potentially dangerous, and safety is of the utmost importance. Major contractors are aware of their responsibilities, and the pilot is in charge of all aspects of the operation involving the helicopter. The pilot will suspend operations if something is unsafe. Elements will include the following:

Safety Briefing

All commercial helicopter operators have a safety section in their operations manual, and all personnel working with a helicopter receive a safety briefing prior to the operation beginning. This usually consists of a verbal briefing on site by the pilot, the purpose being to familiarize staff with their tasks and with safety precautions. The briefing will include:

- Nature, order and weight of loads.
- Method of slinging, hooking and unhooking.
- Use of cargo-hook; warning against inadvertent release.
- Static electricity earthing procedure.
- How to approach, board and exit the helicopter (approach and leave from the front / down slope, operation of door and safety harness).
- Warnings to stand clear of loads during approach, hover and climb.
- Action in the event of emergency landing or release of load.
- Safety clothing to be worn (*see* below).
- Arrangements for refuelling.
- Air/ground/air communications (radios, signals, windsock).

Safety Equipment

All staff on the ground should wear or carry:

- Fluorescent jacket/vest (should be kept fastened to avoid being blown around).

- Safety helmet/ear defenders with chin strap.
- Protective goggles for snow, sandy or dusty environments.
- Electrically resistant gloves (loaders only).
- Steel-toecap boots.
- First aid kit.
- A whistle – useful to attract people's attention over the noise of the helicopter.
- The helicopter company is responsible for providing rescue and fire-fighting equipment.

Person-in-Charge on Site
Decisions about the task are the pilot's responsibility and instructions must be obeyed. A member of staff will be designated as person-in-charge of the lift site, whose responsibilities are to ensure that:

- The weight of the loads does not exceed the maximum weight stipulated by the helicopter company.
- All loads are secure and slung correctly.
- Requirements of the safety briefing are complied with.

Safety Procedures
- Personnel and vehicles not connected with the operation shall be kept clear of the site.
- All personnel and vehicles shall be kept clear of the flight path of slung loads.
- The emergency landing area shall be kept clear.

Fuel Safety
Fuel positioned on site should be secure and away from watercourses and drains.

Fuel is not a great fire hazard, but it should be stored at a safe distance from the operating area and well away from the emergency landing area. Refuelling is carried out by the contractor's own groundcrew.

Conclusion

This just about concludes the health and safety section of this book, although it is by no means an in-depth study. I have only discussed some of the important major aspects of the countryside's working environment, and further information can be sourced from the HSE, whose website is listed at the back of the book.

I will finish here by stating a few more important facts. Most organizations operate a code of practice where people do not work on their own when using power tools or heavy plant; besides, it is much safer to work with a partner anyway.

All working parties must carry a recommended HSE first aid kit, and the kit must be suitable for the number of workers in any given situation. There should be at least one first aider on site at all times. Local authorities are aware of the dangers, so most field workers are trained first aiders anyway.

One very last point to be aware of is that accidents don't just happen: there is always a causative effect that could have been eliminated beforehand.

Sources of Tools and Materials

Unless you are a private individual carrying out minor maintenance on your own land, forget the DIY stores. Most local authorities purchase from bulk suppliers such as dedicated saw mills and, in some cases, farmers' co-operatives. This includes sundry items such as nails, screws and gate fittings – all ironwork for all tasks, in fact. Some authorities and conservation organizations help their local economy by ordering timber from nearby sustainable contacts. Where work tools are concerned, conservation bodies buy them from dedicated suppliers, as they need to be of a high professional standard, able to cope with the continuous day-in, day-out pummelling exerted on them. Many outlets that serve the farming trade hold quantities of professional tools in stock. Cheap imitations are a false, dangerous economy; a claw hammer with a hollow shaft, for example, won't last long before it begins to bend, which usually happens where the head meets the handle after prizing out stubborn, bent nails. Furthermore, working with tools of unsuitable quality has the potential to cause injury.

Drystone walling and stone for bridge abutments, including aggregates for path surfacing, are usually purchased from nearby quarries. For new, large stone projects there is no choice but to import materials from a supplier even if there seems to be an abundance of rock in the vicinity. This rule strongly applies to Sites of Special Scientific Interest (SSSIs) and other sensitive conservation areas where disturbing the ground will have a detrimental effect on the flora and fauna. On sites where no restrictions are in force, it may be possible to source material from the land, but on very large projects it will have a damaging influence locally. The only occasion when it is really safe to exploit existent stone is in the rebuild of stone walls, stiles or similar constructions already featured on the site.

The style of stone you should choose depends on an area's predominant bedrock. The conservation restrictions of the gritstone regions in the Peak District National Park, for instance, demand that all stonework is of native sandstone. In the park's White Peak area, limestone must be used. There are no exceptions, except where the two bedrocks meet. Here you will find drystone walls containing a mixture of sandstone and limestone. Biodiversity and the preservation of local fauna must also be taken into consideration, especially when laying footpath surfaces. Limestone aggregates will change the pH level of acid peat, which could have an unfavourable effect on plant life in close proximity to the path. Disturb the fauna and you may start a detrimental chain reaction in the local biodiversity. This is one reason why national parks and other upland authorities are laying indigenous stone 'causey paths' (explained later).

Where wooden items have to be used you don't really have much choice in the way of bio-friendly wood preservative; the timber is either preserved by additives, or it is not. To install untreated rights-of-way furniture is a false economy, because the items will decay quickly and require replacing. Factory timber treatments could give a gate, stile or footbridge a fifteen- to twenty-year life expectancy; this in itself makes economic sense. There is no doubt that where a wooden post meets the ground a biological change to that immediate vicinity occurs. Unlike footpaths where one could lay in excess of 50 metres of aggregate and cause noticeable shifts, the variation to the base of a finger post is negligible.

CHAPTER 2

UNDERSTANDING RIGHTS OF WAY NAVIGATION

There are many things to consider before commencing work on a public right of way. Perhaps the most important rudimentary skill is knowing how to read a map, and transposing that information to the ground. Many paths marked on the map may not be physically distinguishable in reality, so the ability to work out a definitive line is essential. You will need two items of equipment: a map (of at least 1:25,000 scale) and a good compass with a revolving 'compass housing', usually called a 'bezel', set into a transparent, acrylic protractor or base plate.

Using a Compass

A protractor compass is made up of two parts, one part being the revolving bezel. Inside the bezel is a needle set in liquid. The needle always points towards the magnetic North Pole, known as 'magnetic north'. The north-pointing tip is usually painted red or white. Around the outside of the housing is a set of numbers and letters. The letters, found on the top of the revolving bezel, run in this clockwise order: N, E, S, W, meaning north, east, south and west. Exactly halfway between

the direction letters you may find markings that denote NE, SE, SW, NW, meaning north-east, south-east, south-west and north-west, though a compass is not always marked like this.

On the top of the bezel you will also find a set of numbers, called a scale, ranging from '0' (zero degrees) to '360' (three-hundred-and-sixty degrees); this is called the 'azimuth' or, in navigation terms, a 'bearing'. On the base of the revolving housing there is a set of lines called 'orienting lines', and an arrow called the 'orienting arrow'. The protractor (or base plate) looks very much like a small, wide measuring rule. The protractor has three straight lines running down its length: the two on the outside are for aligning with the 'northing lines' on the OS map, and the one in the centre is called the 'direction-of-travel arrow'; it is this arrow that one follows when walking on a 'bearing'. Most compasses are decorated with inches and centimetres, but the most useful ones have guides to help with reading 'grid references' (explained later).

Let us now try to walk on a bearing of east. First, turn the compass bezel until the 'east' mark is in line with the protractor's direction-of-travel arrow. Second, hold the compass as flat as possible in the palm of one hand, allowing the needle to rotate freely. Maintaining the position of the compass and your hand, turn your body until the painted part of the compass needle is aligned with 'north' (N) on the bezel. The needle should now be resting parallel within the orienting arrow on the base of the housing. Check that the north part of the arrow is actually pointing north, and not south, otherwise you will end up walking in the opposite direction. Magnetic attractions in a local area could give you a false reading, and the same could be said for some items you might be carrying: cell phones, magnets and anything containing iron. This is called 'magnetic deviation'.

Keeping the compass needle at north on the bezel, walk in the direction of the protractor's travel arrow (east). It is difficult to walk whilst looking at a compass, especially over rough terrain, so before you set off, find a fixed point on the near landscape (not an animal or anything else that will move away) that you can align with the direction-of-travel arrow, ensuring that the red needle is still pointing north. When you have walked 25 to 50m, stop and recheck the compass alignment, using the technique just described.

Using a compass on its own, following magnetic north isn't all that accurate because it does not account for 'magnetic declination' and 'true north'. This type of compass exercise is fine if you are

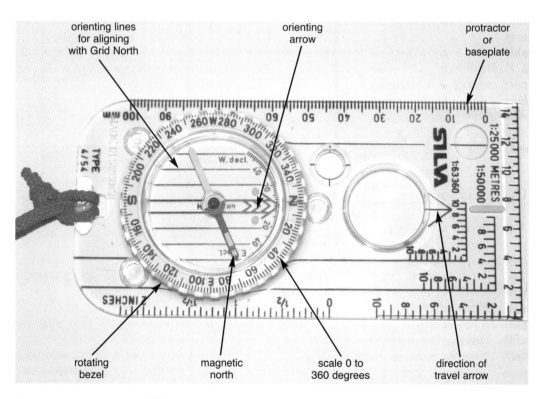

A protractor compass and its parts.

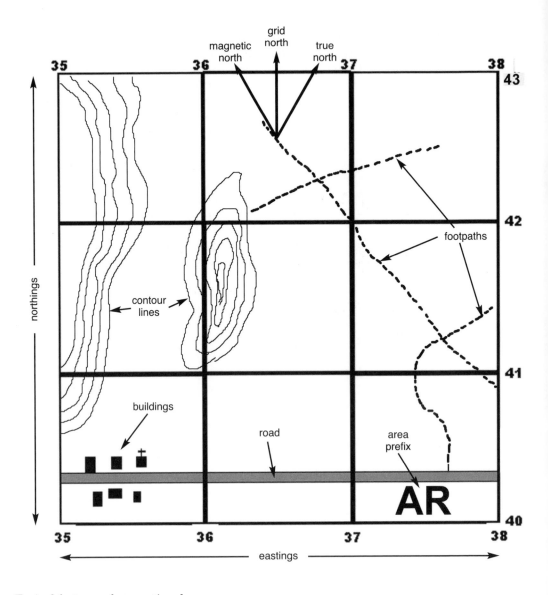

Typical features of conventional maps.

heading towards a road, river or some other long feature. A small site, such as a distant access point on a public right of way, will require precise results, and the best way to do that is by using a map and compass together.

Using a Map

The smallest map you should use for any navigational work is a 1:25,000 Explorer or Pathfinder. It would help if you first familiarized yourself with the map's symbols, for many can be used as navigation aids when travelling through the countryside. To save me going through the entire Ordnance Survey legend catalogue, I will just concentrate on the symbols within this exercise's grid square. Before doing this, however, a brief explanation of grid squares and their numbering is important.

The Ordnance Survey has mapped the entire British Isles, breaking it down into a massive set of 1km by 1km grid squares. Four numbers and a mapping area prefix, such as 'SK', identifies each grid square. A mapping area is a larger square made up of 100 grid squares numbered from 00 to 99 west to east (numbered from left to right on the map), and 00 to 99 south to north (numbered from bottom to top on the map). After that, another 100km mapping area comes into play, numbered in exactly the same fashion, the only change being the prefix. The prefix exists to give each mapping area an individual identifier. The use of the prefix before a six- or eight-figure grid reference will show that the point on the map being referred to is unique: without the prefix that point might just as well be in any mapping area.

So what has all this got to do with erecting a wooden stile in the middle of a field? Wouldn't a spade be more useful? Yes, a spade is important when digging in stile uprights, but knowing the correct grid reference of the access point is essential if you want to do it in the right place. Absolutely everything on a map has its own grid reference, and each 'everything' is made unique by the prefix. A standard grid reference is given with two letters (the prefix) and six numbers, the first three of which are called eastings, and the second three as northings. It should

appear like this: AR 368 (eastings) 423 (northings): AR368423. On the project map this reference refers to a crossroads of footpaths, running across private farmland (it is not a real area, just one made up for this book). Looking at the first two numbers on the eastings and northings – AR36..42.. – tells us the actual name of the grid square we are working on. You can work this out by first reading the eastings (the numbers that run across the bottom or top of a map) and then looking at the northings (the numbers running up the left or right side of the map). Note that the easting 36 begins on the bottom left of the grid square and the northing 42 starts from the lower right.

AR36..42.. only shows a general area, and by breaking the grid square into tenths we can pinpoint an area to within 100m accuracy. You do this by adding a single figure (in increments of tenths) to the easting, and another one to the northing. So, '36' becomes '368' and '42' becomes '423'.

Creating the Six-Figure Grid Reference

The following is a step-by-step method for creating the six-figure grid reference, based on the diagram map depicted in this chapter. First, make sure you can see both easting and northing numbers on the diagram. Next, find easting 36 and place the tip of your finger over the number. For the sake of the exercise this finger has now become the easting finger. Working from left to right, estimate eight-tenths of the grid square and slide your finger to this point. Keeping the easting finger in position, use your other hand to find northing 42. Estimate three-tenths by sliding another finger up the grid square. We will call this the northing finger. To reach the unique point of the grid reference, slide the easting finger up the map, keeping it as straight as possible, and slide the northing finger across the map to meet it. Where your two fingers touch is the grid reference AR368423.

Most professionals, when working on the large definitive maps, go one step further and split the grid square into twentieths to derive a more precise eight-figure grid reference. You can just about achieve this on a 1:25,000 map. Six-figure references will work fine for casual use, but if you need to state the position of a proposed piece of footpath furniture, an eight-figure number will minimize the risk of installing it away from the

definitive line. We will now work this out by using an inexpensive grid reference finder (you can purchase these from most camping and outdoor-leisure retailers). The guide comes with two printed grid squares: large and small. The small square is used to find grid references on 1:50,000 Landranger maps, the large one is used for 1:25,000 maps. The most useful feature on the grid reference finder is that the actual grid-square guides are already separated into tenths, and you only need count the vertical and horizontal lines to create a unique reference. What's more, these guides form even smaller squares that can help to estimate the extra numbers of an eight-figure reference.

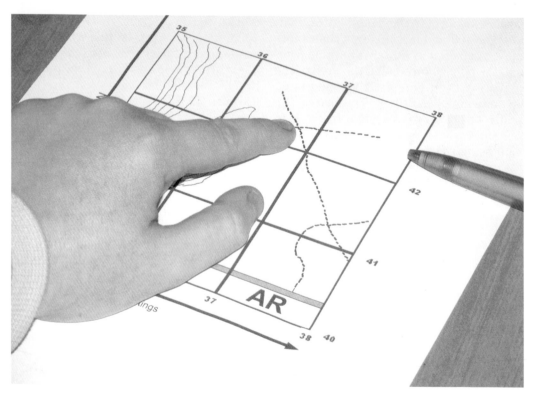

Working out the six-figure grid reference.

We can see that that reference point is actually just before 368; in fact, according to the grid guide, it just falls within the bounds of 367 (remember, an easting is always counted from left to right). Starting from easting 367, estimate how many tenths, within the small square, the crossroads are located: the answer is nine. So, in the context of an eight-figure grid reference, our easting has now become 3679. Repeating this procedure for the northing 423, we can see that the reference point just falls within the scope of 422, and an estimation (by counting the guide's smaller squares) transposes the northing into an actual 4228. We have now formulated an almost exact unique grid reference for the path crossroads, namely AR36794228.

Interpreting Height on a Map

You can work out an accurate position for a proposed work project by creating a grid reference, but what if the work involves some footpath repair on a dangerous section of high ground? The ability to understand how height is recorded on a map is important. Upland paths may have vertical sections or treacherous areas of ground close to the work site. The practical problems of transporting materials and tools to a site will be affected by the lie of the land, and many of today's existing upland path projects require the use of a helicopter for airlifting supplies.

An Ordnance Survey map uses contour lines to show rising and falling land. All

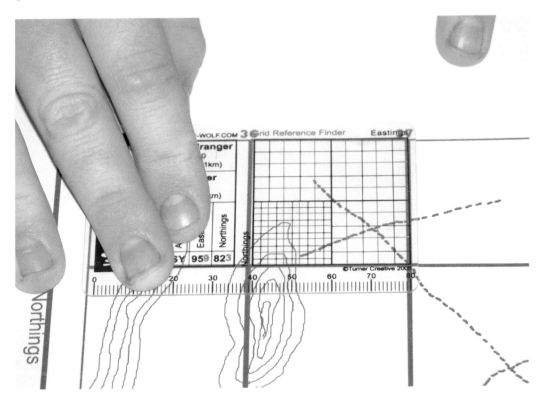

Placing the grid-reference finder on the grid square.

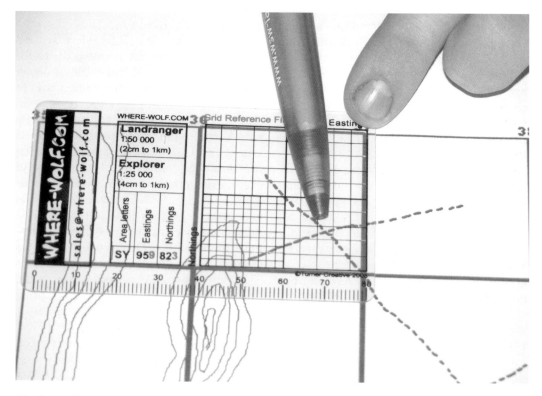

Each small square represents a tenth of a grid square. To estimate an eight-figure reference, break the smaller square into tenths as well.

height above sea level is represented by contours, and the closer they are together, the steeper is the ground. Not only can you use contours to gauge gradients, you can use them to calculate the height of any given point on a hill. The latter is made easy by the fact that a single contour, regardless of shape, is the same height above sea level no matter how far one can trace its route with a finger. On 1:50,000 and 1:25,000 maps the contours are 10m apart. To indicate whether the gradient is falling or rising, the height is shown at regular intervals, usually every 25m to 50m. If there are no numbers on the section of map covering your area the gradient can be worked out one of two ways. One method is to trace a finger over a line until you see a nearby height figure; however, this method can prove fairly tedious. The second is to find the darker, bold contours, because these lines, called 'index contours', are always spaced at 50m intervals.

The Shape of the Ground

Not only can contours explain the slope of the landscape, they can also demonstrate the shape of the ground. When the ground turns into a valley, the contours will form a 'V' or 'U' shape. A 'V'-shaped valley has steep sides, and a 'U'-shaped one has gentle, easy aspects. A group of contours that form a close, circular pattern, wider at the edge and finishing with a smaller ring in the middle, denotes a conical hill, if the height figures are ascending towards the smaller circle. A cluster of fairly long, straight contours with a wide summit shows a plateau; and if these contours are very close together, the slope leading up to the plateau is steep. If all the contour lines appear to change direction after running north, let's say to the left of the map, it shows that the hill bends towards the west.

This may seem complicated at first, but it shouldn't take long to get the hang of it. The best way to look at contour lines is by going to a hilly location and studying the ground and map at the same time.

Using a Map and Compass together

The combination of map and compass is the most important navigation technique, though there are many things to consider before pointing the compass and attempting to walk to your destination. The difference between 'grid north', 'magnetic north' and 'true north' plays a significant role when walking on a bearing. Thus, magnetic north is where the compass needle points to, grid north runs from the bottom to the top of the map, and true north is the direction to the geographic North Pole, the point of the earth's axis rotation.

A compass needle does not actually point to the North Pole; it aligns itself with the earth's magnetic field, which, from Britain's perspective, is west of magnetic north. This variation is called the 'declination'. To make matters more complicated, the earth's magnetic poles

are constantly moving – be it slowly – over many years, in a diameter of around 160km (100 miles). As a result, the declination changes too. When taking a bearing from the map, the protractor is aligned with a proposed route and the bezel orienting arrow is turned to align with the map's grid lines – grid north. To adjust for the declination you must turn the bezel anti-clockwise. In Britain the declination is around 6 degrees west of magnetic north, but the actual amount is dependent on location. All Ordnance Survey maps contain the correct declination information for any given mapping area, and it is best to check this first.

Working with the project map, we are now going to navigate to the crossroads at AR36794228 by following the marked footpaths. From the road's access point, at grid reference AR37654035, follow the well marked path until you reach the crossroads at AR37624121. Let us assume there is a fingerpost at this intersection, pointing towards the general area of the path. We can tell by the post (and looking at the map) that the direction of the second crossroads is northwest, but the path isn't visible on the land. The problem is, we need to walk the definitive line to stay within the law, and we also have to reach our destination accurately. This is when the use of the compass is essential.

Lay the protractor of the compass on the map. Next, align the side of the protractor against the line of the footpath, ensuring that it bisects the start point (the fingerpost) and the end point (the second crossroads). The direction-of-travel arrow should now be pointing towards NW. Keeping the compass in position, turn the bezel until the 'orienting arrow' points grid north. After you have done

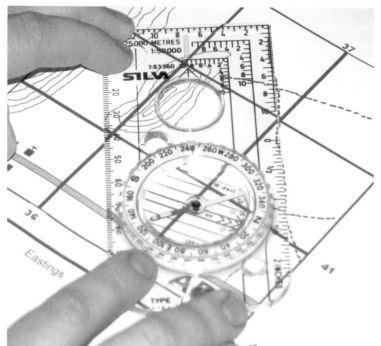

The compass is aligned with the direction of travel.

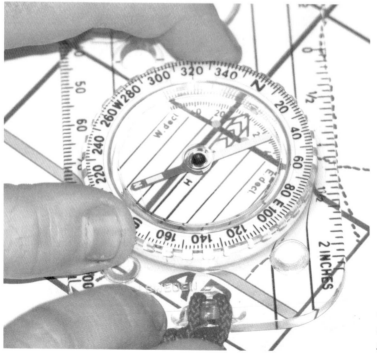

Turn the bezel until the orienting arrow points to grid north.

*This is the magnetic
north bearing of 320
degrees.*

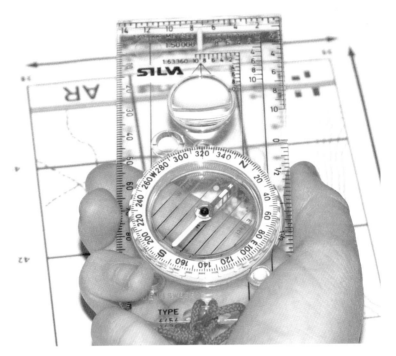

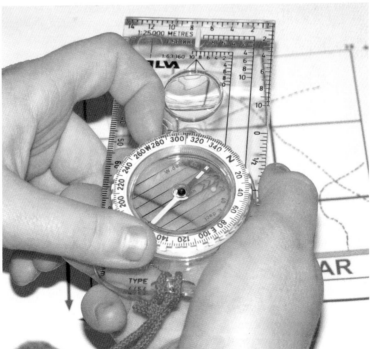

*Turn the bezel
anticlockwise to adjust
for magnetic declination.*

Whilst holding the compass level, turn your body until the red north arrow is aligned with the orienting arrow. Now you can walk on the bearing.

this, take the compass off the map and adjust for the declination; on our map it is 6 degrees west. This means you will have to rotate the bezel 6 degrees in an anti-clockwise direction. (For your information, the scale on most compasses rises every two degrees, 2, 4, 6, 8 and so on.)

Making sure you don't maladjust the bezel, hold the compass flat, in the palm of your hand. Now rotate your body until the red part of the needle is parallel within the orienting arrow. The actual bearing is 320 degrees; after adjusting for declination it is 314 degrees.

I am now going to confuse you even further. The last exercise dealt with taking a compass bearing from a map, adjusting for the declination, and turning it into a direction to walk in. When this is done in the opposite way, taking a bearing from a point on the ground and transposing it to the map, the declination has to be adjusted clockwise. The best way to explain this is by using the bearing of 314 degrees explained earlier. If the compass is still set at 314 degrees, place it on the map and align the bezel's orienting arrow with grid north. Do not rotate the bezel: turn the protractor instead. You will notice that the side of the protractor is not accurately aligned with the footpath. Take the compass away from the map and rotate the bezel 6 degrees clockwise. Now return it to the map, aligning the orienting arrow with grid north, by adjusting the whole compass, not the bezel. The path is now aligned.

CHAPTER 3

ACCESS FOR ALL

Walking Britain's public rights-of-way network is one of our common pastimes. For numerous years vast tracts of land have remained inaccessible to a large section of society; but happily this is slowly changing. Local authorities, national parks and other countryside organizations are adopting policies in accordance with the Disabilities Discrimination Act 1995 (DDA), and although they are not bound by law to cater for disabilities on most countryside routes, they are instigating voluntary codes of practice in an attempt to open up the countryside for path users with physical and motor disabilities. In the past, when dealing with footpath access, the first and only solution was to erect a wooden or stone stile. This, I am happy to say, has changed, and nowadays countryside managers adopt what is known as the 'least restrictive option' (LRO).

New footpath projects are initially viewed from a standpoint of 'access for all'. When surveying proposed rights-of-way work, the primary priority is to the ability of the path user. Gates, for example, have replaced stiles as the preferred means of passing through access points because they are easier to negotiate, and they have opened up vast areas of countryside otherwise inaccessible to people with disabilities. Across Britain many existing stiles have been dismantled and gates hung in their place. This is not to say that wooden and stone stiles do not have an important function, and they are still an integral part of the rights-of-way network; if the terrain is found unsuitable for wheelchairs, or the landowner doesn't like the idea of a gate, the next 'least restrictive option' comes into the scenario. This could mean the construction of a wider stile, with three treads instead of two.

New path-resurfacing strategies are considered in the same light. The maximum gradient for wheelchairs and invalid carriages is 1 in 10, and if the project's terrain falls within this parameter, then the 'least restrictive option' must consider these users. Further equal and important factors include people with visual and hearing impairments, or with motor disabilities, and those who do not need a wheelchair but have difficulty walking.

LRO is an exciting philosophy that successfully attempts to obtain a balance between path-user interests. The difficult-to-climb, stone step-over stile is now the least desirable option (although I still love building them), but this is no bad thing if more people can enjoy and respect the land.

To start the practical section of this book I have included in this chapter a step-by-step photo project of a kissing gate, a picket gate, and a gate for accessing a bridleway. Easy-to-follow instructions are included in their relevant captions.

Kissing Gate

A kissing gate is an ideal alternative to a stock-proof stile or a standard access gate that relies on a clasp to ensure animals can't escape. Kissing gates, if built correctly, offer stock proofing by default, and at the same time allow comfortable passage through a field boundary. The following project was carried out by an organization called 'Countryside Skills' for Denbighshire Countryside Service.

Building a Kissing Gate

The following sequence of illustrations sets out the basics of building a kissing gate.

This material is locally sourced, sustainable hardwood; 7ft × 4in × 4in (2.1m × 10cm × 10cm) posts, 4in × 2in (10cm × 5cm) rails and one 3ft (1m) gate. You will also need 5in (12cm) galvanized nails, fencing staples and a gate-hanging kit.

Before work starts, the ground surrounding the gate must be levelled. Raised ground that could be hazardous to users passing through, must be smoothed down. This is also essential for the gate's free travel when opening and closing.

The best method of working out the feature's position is to align the gate roughly where it will hang on the completed structure. Mark the area where the hanging post (or stoop) should be dug in.

First, dig the posthole for the gate hanger using a crowbar to loosen stone and soil, lifting out the spoil with a spade. The posthole must be at least 2ft (60cm) deep, with enough width to allow the insertion of medium-sized rock around the buried timber.

Testing the depth of the posthole. At the moment it is not deep enough.

As soon as you have reached the required depth, firm in the gate stoop by applying alternate layers of soil and rock, and compacting down with each tier.

All posts must be vertical, so it is important to keep checking the levels at all times.

After completion of the gate stoop, you can now attach the gate's hinge kit. You will need to pre-drill every hole.

The best way to work out the position of the hinges is to clamp the actual 'hinge band' to the gate, then mark through the holes with a pencil. After drilling, tap the bolts through using a hammer, and then tighten with nuts and washers on the other side.

Drilling the bottom of the gate for the lower hinge.

Tightening and adjusting the gate's lower hinge.

The next job is to work out where the 'clapper post' should go. This is easily done by swinging the gate until it is running in a straight line with the stoop. Bring the clapper flush and vertical with the gate end, and mark the posthole's position on the ground. When closed, the gate should rest against the back of the clapper.

After firming in the clapper post, work out the position for the second clapper post. Starting at the first clapper, swing the gate in a 90-degree arc and then mark the position for the second one. Next, mark the positions for the last two posts. These are the ones that give a kissing gate a box-like appearance. As a rule, the distance between all posts should be the same as the gate's length. Sometimes this may not possible. If this is the case you can set the last ones in closer together, but the distance from each clapper post must be at least 3ft (90cm).

The last phase of the job is to attach the stock-proofing rail. Complete one side first. Nail the bottom rails 2–3in (5–7.5cm) above the ground. The gap between the first and second rail should be no more than 4in (10cm) to take account of lambs in the spring. From this point the rail gaps can be increased until you reach the top course.

When you have railed one side, a spirit level can be used as an aid for the remaining timber.

Trim all the posts to within 1in or so above the rail. Note the angle of cut. This allows rainwater to flow easily off the post. Always create an angle away from fixings, or where rails abut timber.

The completed kissing gate.

Simple Access Gate

The 'least restrictive option' was applied to this following example carried out by the Peak District National Park Authority's countryside maintenance team. The project involved taking down an existing stone stile and replacing it with a lightweight picket gate.

Building a Simple Access Gate

The following sequence of illustrations sets out the basics of building a simple access gate.

Excavate the posthole for the gate stoop as described for the kissing gate. The tool depicted here is called a 'shoeveholer', and is ideal for lifting spoil out of deep holes.

Fill the posthole by packing alternate layers of stone and soil around the gate stoop.

Test the gatepost by pushing and pulling with your hand. If excess movement is detected, the stoop will require re-packing.

Now that the gate stoop is firmly in the ground, the gate's hinges can be attached. The next job is to fix the gate hangers to the stoop. Align the gate with the post to work out the position of the top hanger. Ensure there is enough ground clearance for the gate to travel freely without compromising stock proofing.

The top hanger should be aligned vertically, and screwed to the centre of the stoop. You will find the next stage easier if the hanger's pin is pointing upwards, like the one in the photograph.

Screwing the hanger to the gate stoop.

Hang the gate on the top hanger, then use a spirit level to align it correctly. Having done this, you can now mark the position for the bottom gate hanger. Whilst someone is supporting the gate, just drop the hanger pin through the hinge part and let it rest. If the lower hanger's pin points towards the ground, the gate cannot be lifted off accidentally or otherwise.

Attaching the lower hanger can be done with the gate in position.

You can't guarantee that walkers will close a gate, but you can make a gate close automatically, and a heavy-duty gate spring will do this for you. First, you will need to drill a pilot hole through the lower section of the gate. Do this by aligning the spring, at roughly 45 degrees, with the gate and the stoop. The gate should be in its closed position, with the spring's lowest end placed against the stoop. Mark and drill the gate and stoop for bolts.

This bolt is ready to be tapped through with a hammer.

Secure the bolt with a nut and washer.

Drilling the gate stoop for the spring.

Secure another bolt, and then lock it off with a nut and washer.

The finished gate spring.

A simple cabin hook for added stock proofing. This is only good for sheep; equines and bovines will require a stronger clasp.

It is a good idea to add a sign reminding walkers to fasten the gate.

The second phase of the job is to rebuild the wall end, although this can be done at the same time as hanging the gate if there are enough people in the work party. The photograph shows the wall's foundations being prepared.

This through-stone has been laid on the existing foundation stones.

A wall end is built using through-stones and runners (explained later).

Laying the top stones (called 'coping', explained later).

The finished project. The addition of a small post-and-rail fence guarantees that no stock can escape.

Bridle Gate

The only type of access furniture you should install on bridleways is a gate. Most equine access points require a maximum width, so the longer the feature, the better; a gate measuring 6ft (1.8m) should be your absolute minimum. Bridle gates can be designed to open whilst the rider is mounted. In most circumstances, riders dismount, open the access point and walk the animal through. But what happens if the horse is difficult to mount, or the rider is unable to mount unaided?

Operating a gate equipped with a standard 'auto latch' can sometimes prove awkward when one is trying to control an excited animal, and even more so when the latch is fixed to the opposite side.

The next set of photographs shows the Peak Park's countryside maintenance team installing a new field gate, complete with bridle-latch, a device that enables a rider to open the access point without dismounting. We pick up the project after the stoop and clapper post have been firmed in (this technique has already been described for the kissing gate).

After firming in a 7ft × 8in × 7in (2.1m × 20cm × 17cm) gate stoop to a depth of at least 3ft (90cm), the bridle gate can be hung.

A clapper post of similar size and depth is installed, then an equine-friendly bridle latch is affixed with coach screws.

A large catch is then attached to the front of the gate.

The bridle gate in its closed position.

The bridle latch in operation.

CHAPTER 4

REVETMENT BOARDING

Revetments are used to retain soil on paths that run parallel to a slope or follow a route contouring a hill. As a path wears, the walking surface begins to break down. On flat ground this eventually produces a widening, muddy track, mainly because walkers tend to avoid wet sections and walk on the drier land on either side (explained in detail in Chapter 11). On paths where the terrain rises steeply on one side and falls sharply on the other there tends to be no mud-avoidance option, so the path becomes more worn as time goes by. Eventually it becomes so eroded that the surface begins to fall away on the downhill side, and in some cases an earth wall starts to appear on the uphill side. As there is nothing containing the land on this higher section, rain and water run-off will wash the soil on to the path so the earth bank becomes more eroded. This, in turn, weakens the structure of the lower section.

The project for this chapter describes an advanced technique for the downhill side, and a standard method for containing earth on the upland section. We will assume the route is heavily used and a 10ft (3m) length of path requires repair. The original width of the path is around 2ft (60cm).

The job will involve a complete rebuild of the entire eroded walking surface. Being a popular tourist area, the path has to sustain heavy visitor traffic, so the lower section must physically be able to cope with the burden. The displacement and compression caused by the weight of each footfall needs to be dispersed as evenly as possible. Displacement occurs on both sides of the path, but it is the outer, downhill part where most of the damage happens. The objective is to construct a feature that will hold the path surface securely in situ. Even with revetment boarding, dislocation of the track may occur, causing the boards to splay outwards. This effect can be reduced by securing the boards with windlasses (explained later).

Repairing the Lower Section

Materials Required

The following materials are just a guide, and are listed to give an idea of the requirements, as many projects like this sometimes rely on the availability of suitable matter within a locality. The following construction guide, however, is accurate.

- 5 × 10ft × 6in × 2in (3.1m × 15cm × 5cm) treated wooden boards.
- 13 × 5ft × 3.5in (1.5m × 9cm) round, pointed fencing stakes.
- 1 roll of low-tensile fencing wire.
- Galvanized nails.
- Fencing staples.
- Around 3 tonnes of aggregates or large stone.
- Around 1 tonne of top-surface stone.

Tool Requirements

How many of each tool you will need will depend on the size of the work party.

- Claw hammer.
- Wire cutters.
- Fencing pliers.
- Pick.
- Mattock.
- Fencing maul (you can use a post slammer as an alternative, but there are a few safety issues to remember. Do not lift the tool higher than the post, as it could glance off the top and recoil towards the user. Head protection must be worn at all times for this reason).
- Sledgehammer.
- Crowbar.
- Tamper.
- Rake.
- Hand saw.
- Spirit level.
- Tape measure.
- Hand drill (a rechargeable drill is the ideal alternative).
- Torsion bar (this is for turning the low-tensile wire to create 'windlasses'. Ideally the bar should be solid steel, between 8 to 10in (20 to 25cm) long, and about 1in (13mm) in diameter).
- Wheelbarrow.

- Safety glasses or goggles (part of the task involves breaking large stones with a sledgehammer, which will cause shards of rock to fly in random directions. It is for this reason that eye protection must be worn).

Preparing the Eroded Path

The first task is to slightly widen the eroded area by cutting away the earth wall on the uphill side of the path. At first this may seem to be defeating the object of the repair, but the extra width will allow room for the windlass anchors so they don't encroach on the finished walking surface. Eventually the uphill revetments will hide these stakes. You should only need to dig back about 6in (15cm), or until a straight face of firm soil has been achieved.

Next, concentrate on the eroded path surface. When the new path section is finished it should be the same level as the existing track on either side, but the damaged section must be dug out first. I would suggest an excavation 6in to 8in (15 to 20cm) deep, down the whole eroded site. It would also be a good idea to find a nearby storage location for the spoil.

The next job is to prepare the downhill edge for the revetment boards. At least half of the baseboard's height, which equates to 3in (8cm), should be placed against firm earth with the bottom of the board resting on a level, stable foundation. Using a spade, shave at least 2in (5cm) of soil from the entire edge, taking it down to around 3in (8cm), then level it with a tamper. At this point I would usually suggest checking the foundation with a long spirit level. This is fine if the worksite is on level ground, but not if the path is going uphill. If you can use a level,

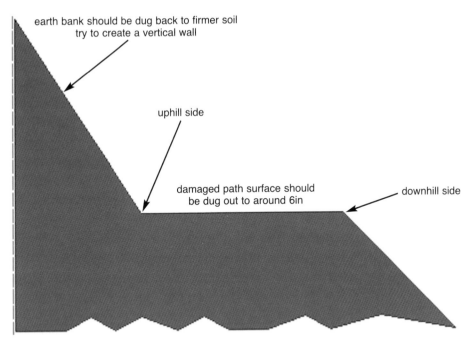

Repairing a damaged path section with revetment boarding – step 1.

earth bank should be dug back to firmer soil
try to create a vertical wall

uphill side

damaged path surface should
be dug out to around 6in

downhill side

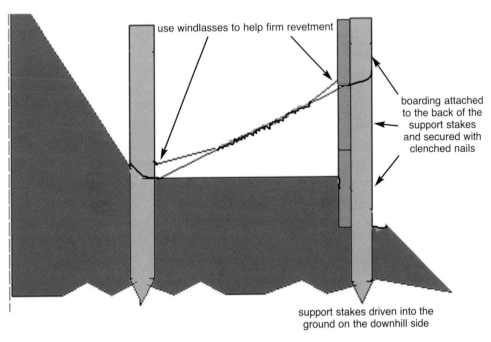

Repairing a damaged path section with revetment boarding – step 2.

use windlasses to help firm revetment

boarding attached
to the back of the
support stakes
and secured with
clenched nails

support stakes driven into the
ground on the downhill side

that's great, otherwise check the depth, on both ends and in the middle, with a tape measure.

Laying the Boarding

With the excavation work complete, it is now time to start laying the boarding. Take one 10ft (3m) board (the baseboard) and lay it on its longer 2in (5cm) edge, against the side of the newly excavated section that was shaved off the path edge. To ensure the board is resting firmly on the foundation area, gently tap it down with a fencing maul.

The next phase will require a second person to hold the board in place whilst another inserts supporting stakes. You will need at least three 5ft (1.5m) stakes to help support the revetment, two at either end and one in the middle, and on

heavy-duty constructions such as this I prefer to use five, as it will reduce the risk of the wood bulging and splitting in the future when the path settles.

With the board held in place, measure and scribe three easily definable marks every 2ft (60cm) along the top edge of the board. These markers are guides for the five supporting stakes; you can exploit each end of the board as guides for the two end stakes. Before inserting stakes, it is advisable to make five deep, vertical pilot holes (or postholes) with the crowbar. With pre-bored postholes there is less chance of the posts veering at an angle when you hammer them into the ground. Take the crowbar and align it vertically with one of the board ends, then adjust it until at least 2in (5cm) of the board end overlaps the bar. The supporting stakes are secured to the outside

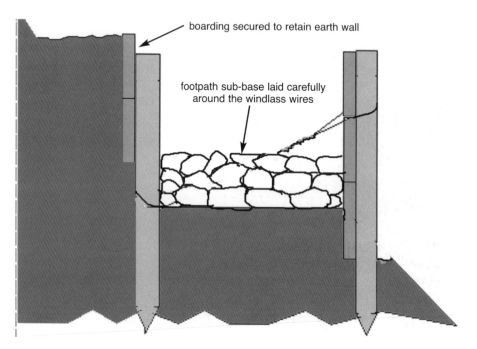

boarding secured to retain earth wall

footpath sub-base laid carefully around the windlass wires

Repairing a damaged path section with revetment boarding – step 3.

of the revetment, so ensure the crowbar is aligned accordingly. Holding the crowbar as vertically as possible, ram it hard into the ground, then turn it 360 degrees. Then lift the bar out and repeat the action – on this occasion it will penetrate deeper. Continue like this until you have achieved a 1ft (30cm) depth. If the post-hole can go any deeper, take it down to a depth of 2ft (60cm).

Having done this, go to the opposite end of the board and repeat the method just described. To create the three inner postholes, just align the bar with the scribe marks (made earlier) and repeat the crowbar action again.

You will now have to hammer in the supporting stakes. Working from one end, manually ram a stake into the posthole and adjust it until it is vertical. If you are using a post slammer it will be fairly easy

to sustain alignment as you push the stake into the ground.

Working with a fencing maul requires more accuracy. To avoid splitting the wood or missing the stake completely, the full striking face of the tool must be applied. This means that every post thump must be made with the tool held horizontal. It's not easy at first, considering the maul is lowered in an arc, but it is a technique that has to be mastered, and it takes time to achieve precision. You can practise by first resting the full striking area on the top of the post. Gripping the shaft of the maul with two hands (similar to the way one holds a rifle), raise the tool about 5in (13cm), holding it horizontal at all times, then rest it back on the post. Carry on doing this until you find the confidence to lift the maul higher and bring it down more firmly. Soon the technique

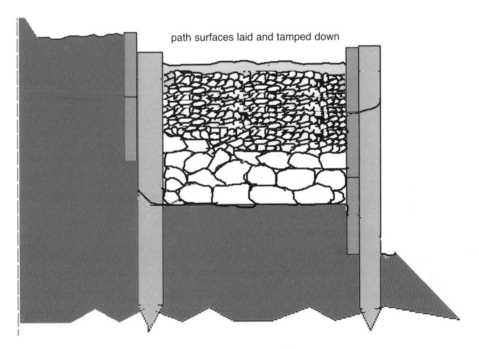

path surfaces laid and tamped down

Repairing a damaged path section with revetment boarding – step 4.

will become second nature, and stamina will improve.

The stakes should be abutting the board when they are driven home; the last thing you want is a gap in between. To guarantee a close fit, stand on the path with the boarding and post in front of you. There is a good reason for this, because the natural arc of the maul, when falling, will tend to force the stake towards the user. In some cases this could be a hindrance, on revetment tasks it works to your advantage. Nonetheless, there is always a risk that the post will glance off a stone and begin to veer sideways, so for added security someone could brace the post against the board with a heavy tool such as a sledgehammer or crowbar. The stake should be driven down as far it can go, or until it is so firm that strong pushing or pulling will not cause misalignment.

Drive in the remaining four posts using the technique just described. Unfortunately, due to the nature of the ground, buried stone is unavoidable and there is always a risk the stake will angle slightly to left or right.

Fixing the Baseboard

Before continuing, grub out a section of soil behind each stake and the board, on the path side; this is so that the 6in (15cm) nail points will be exposed after they are driven home. Next, with a hand drill or rechargeable drill, bore ten pilot holes through the stakes and into the board (two holes for each stake, one above the other, 2in (5cm) apart).

Working from the downhill side, drive ten 6in nails into the support stakes until their points are poking through the board. The baseboard should now be held

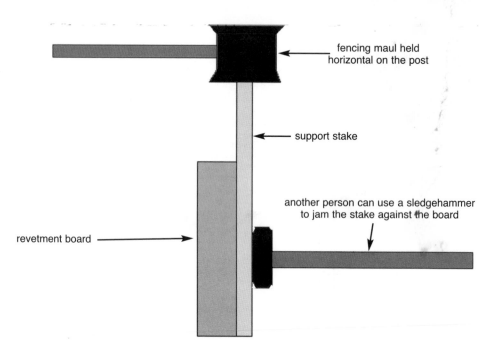

fencing maul held
horizontal on the post

support stake

another person can use a sledgehammer
to jam the stake against the board

revetment board

Knocking in support stakes.

securely. For added stability, bend (or clench) the nail points to the back of the board, using the hammer. This simple action will stop the revetment drifting away from the stakes as the path settles and compacts in the future. The last job here is to replace the soil in the holes made for exposing the nail ends.

The second revetment board can now be laid on top of the baseboard by following the method just described.

Making the Windlasses

You will need to drive in five posts (windlass anchors) near the earth wall at the back of the path (the uphill area), and each of these posts must be approximately in line with a support stake at the front; you can judge their positions by eye. Bore postholes and drive the anchors home working to the same technique described earlier. Usually, windlass anchors are driven in at an angle. However, this will most likely be impossible when working against an earth wall. It is important, then, to drive the posts in as deep as possible.

Measure the distance between the anchors and support stakes, and treble it. Next, transfer this measurement to a length of low tensile fencing wire and cut it away from the roll. Working from one of the support stakes, fix an end of the wire to the stake by hammering in a fencing staple. Ensure the wire is touching the top edge of the revetment board. Next, take the wire down to the opposite windlass anchor and attach it at ground level by driving in a further staple, but allow a slight clearance between staple and wire. Now tension the wire, either by hand or

boards secured to the back of the stakes

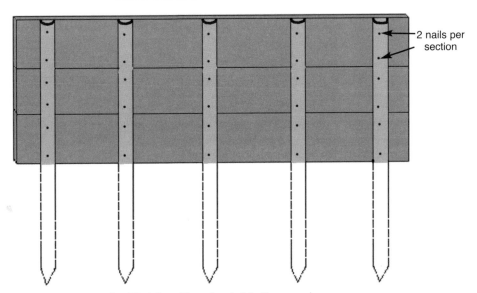

2 nails per section

5 × 5ft stakes driven deeply into the ground

Method for attaching support stakes and boards on the downhill side.

by using the fencing pliers. Whilst maintaining this strain, drive the staple home. Bring the wire back up to the support stake, ensuring it is touching the top edge of the board, then tension it and connect it to the post. Repeat this procedure for all the remaining supports and anchors.

It is now time to tension each windlass in turn. Starting with the most central support stake and anchor, take the torsion bar and insert it between the two wires, somewhere near the centre. Twist the bar so that the two wires begin to overlap, and continue twisting until the revetment support stake begins to move towards its anchor. Before removing the bar, carefully guide it back in the opposite direction; this should be around half a turn. Now, tighten the last four windlasses using the method just described. The entire revetment should now be solid and

immovable. Before connecting the top board, using the method described earlier, saw the windlass anchors close to ground level.

Repairing the Uphill Section

The Earth Wall Revetment

This next phase of the work deals with the revetment to the earth wall on the uphill side of the path. To begin, place a new section of 10ft (3m) board against the earth wall on the uphill side, bringing it as level as you can with the new revetment. For the time being we are only using this as a guide for the postholes. With the crowbar, bore out just three postholes as described earlier, one hole

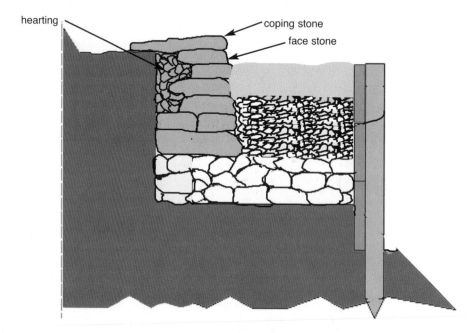

You can build a dry stone retaining wall on the uphill side if the material is available.

for each on each end, and another in the middle. Next, drive in three stakes as far as they will go, then remove the board and put it to one side.

Before connecting the revetment here, place a large rock subsurface on to the path. Ideally the stone should be packed above the join of the revetment's baseboard and second board. Particular attention must be paid to the windlass anchors and wire: rather than just throwing stone

at these features, carefully place it against them. Level off the path as much as you can by breaking the top layer of stone with a sledgehammer. This will also have the secondary benefit of plugging the gaps between the large rocks.

Now we can affix the last revetment boards. Although it is good practice to connect the timber behind support stakes, it may not be possible due to landscape obstructions such as tree roots or

Wooden revetment on a sloping path.

large boulders. Unlike the first section where strength and support was vital, the boards here are not weight-bearing, but are merely there to act as barriers against weather erosion, so three posts instead of five are sufficient.

Surfacing the Path

The last phase of the project deals with laying the path's secondary subsurface and top surface. Aggregate or smaller stone should now be brought in, and every barrowload raked level. As soon as a layer of aggregate covers the base rocks, the entire 10ft (3m) length should be compacted with a tamper. A second layer can now be loaded in and compacted. Continue in this fashion until the path surface is raised to around 3 to 4in (8 to

10cm) above the join of the second and top board on the downhill side.

To finish the project, import another layer of aggregates to the uphill side of the path, then rake it towards the outer revetment, only this time try to create a slight cross-fall (angle the path surface down and away from the hillside). Doing this will direct rainwater downhill and off the path. The top aggregates can now be imported, tamping down each layer. Continue in this fashion until the surface on the downhill side is level with the top edge of the board. For an aesthetic look, trim the tops of each post to the level of their respective boards.

As walkers use the path, the stone will settle and compact even further. As a result, you may need to dress the top surface one more time. Aggregates are discussed in greater detail in Chapter 12.

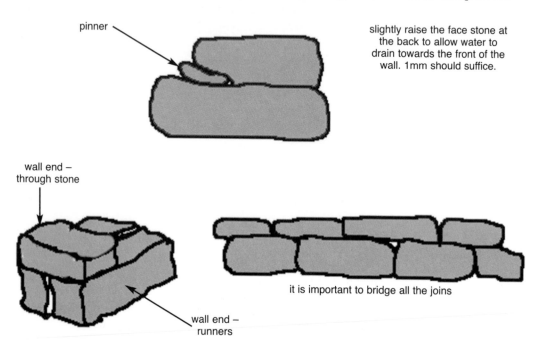

Some important walling techniques.

CHAPTER 5

NATURAL STONE REVETMENTS

Not only do natural features appear pleasing to the eye, they are much better at blending with the surrounding landscape. Many stone revetments are built as 'wet-stone retaining walls', meaning they are held together with sand and cement. This is a strong, lasting technique only if the structure can rest on very solid foundations, where the ground underneath won't give way under the weight, or draining water will not undermine or 'scour' the foundation stones. Wet-stone revetments are ideal for repairing long stretches of path adjacent to eroded riverbanks, or to control erosion of a bare earth slope. For small areas, similar to the outer revetment (the downhill side) described in Chapter 4, they are, in my opinion, unsuitable. The path here was heavily used, and over time the stones would have become unstable as people walked over them. Nonetheless, a stone revetment would have worked on Chapter 4's uphill, earth bank and this chapter replaces the boarding with a *dry-stone* version.

Why dry stone as opposed to wet stone? The simple answer is that dry-stone walls, if built correctly, are durable and can last many years. Furthermore, if you understand the pattern of their construc-

tion, the transition to natural, wet-stone walling will be easy. They are, in fact, comparable in building style down to the last small stone, the only obvious difference being sand and cement. If you do not comprehend the dry-stone technique, you will risk using too much mortar filling, and not enough stone. Mortar will crack and turn to rubble in frosty conditions, and if there is nothing else reinforcing the stone, the wall will eventually collapse.

It is therefore best to start by briefly explaining what a dry-stone wall actually is. If you would like to read an in-depth study and practical guide, my book *A Guide to Dry Stone Walling* (Crowood, 2001) details many aspects of the craft. There are two kinds of dry-stone wall: a single-sided or 'single-skinned' retaining wall (the project for this chapter), and a double-skinned boundary wall. Like a standard brick-mortared wall, a dry-stone wall sits on a firm foundation, it has a succession of interlocking layers called 'courses' that give it height, and it is secured by top stones, usually called 'coping' or 'copeing'. The similarity ends here. Where a brick wall relies on sand and cement for stability, the structural integrity of a dry-stone wall is sustained by varying sizes of strategically placed rock.

Dry-stone walls, whether single- or double-skinned, host the same features: they both rest on a base of large foundation stones; above these, courses of intermediate stones called 'face-stones' are laid. Small rocks called 'pinning' are inserted behind the face-stones to immobilize any detrimental movement that could otherwise cause the wall to collapse. In between the skins of a two-sided boundary wall, smaller rock, called 'hearting', is carefully slotted into every gap and crevice. On a retaining wall the hearting is inserted between the face-stones and earth bank. The last course of wall, the coping, helps to tie the two skins together or, in the case of a retaining wall, secure it to the earth bank. Coping has another important attribute in that it helps to deflect the eroding behaviour of rainwater and frost.

Another important feature on a dry-stone wall is the 'batter'. The retaining wall's batter causes the structure to lean into the area it is designed to protect. On a double-skinned version this lean culminates in the wall appearing triangular if looked at from one end. This lean is vital as it helps to disperse the weight of each face stone towards the firm foundations at ground level. If a wall is built without a batter there is every chance it will topple over.

A wall can not rely on its batter alone; the techniques used to lay stone are of structural importance also. One can't just drop rock and hope to produce a long-lasting feature; each stone has to be laid correctly if the structure is going to withstand the trials of nature, animals and climbing humans. The following project is a step-by-step guide to building a dry-stone retaining wall; as I have mentioned earlier, it may replace the revetment installed on the uphill side of the path described in Chapter 4.

Material Requirements

Work on the principle of 0.5 tonnes of random stone for every 1 metre of retaining wall built to a 4ft (1.2m) height. Incidentally, on a double-skinned wall this will equate to 1 tonne per metre.

Tool Requirements

- Walling hammer: this tool is similar to a lump hammer and is designed for breaking and shaping stone. Walling hammers come in different sizes and weights, but they all have a blunt end for breaking, and a chisel end for shaping and cutting.
- Sledgehammer.
- Crowbar.
- Batter frame: a device used to help achieve the wall's important structural lean. On double-skinned walls, the batter frame is shaped like an 'A', as this helps to form both of the faces. For retaining walls, 4ft (1.2m) steel rods can be used instead. We will use two batter rods for our 10ft section of wall. As a matter of interest, for longer sections it is advisable to insert a third rod, somewhere in the middle, to stop the string sagging. Extensive sections will require more.
- Nylon string-line: used in conjunction with the batter frames as a guide to creating a smooth-faced wall.
- Bucket: ideal for collecting hearting.
- Line-level: a small spirit level that hangs on a string-line. Aligning string-lines correctly helps to produce

aesthetically pleasing, level walls.
- Wheelbarrow: for moving stone around the work site, and for storing large quantities of hearting.
- Safety glasses or goggles.
- Leather safety gloves: the abrasive nature of stone will shred rubber gloves.

Method of Construction

Preparing and Laying Foundations

Usually the first job before building any dry-stone wall is to 'grade' stone. Grading is a process of sourcing material for foundations, coping, intermediate face stone, through-stones and runners (explained later in this chapter). The second and third tasks are to set up a batter frame and string-line, then excavate a foundation trench. In the case of our project wall a foundation already exists, in that the eroded path surface has already been dug out and the outer revetment boards have now been secured to the downhill side. The only change you will need to apply is the size of the stone at the base of the earth wall: instead of large, random-shaped rocks, a strong course of substantial, wide and high heavy stone should be laid. Ideally these stones should be weighty enough to sit on the foundation base without moving or rocking from side to side. With that in mind, the bottom of the rock has to have a surface area broad enough to enable it to rest independently.

The top surface of the foundation is also important, because you will have to lay stones on top of it. Any acute angles that slope towards the outside of the wall will cause the stone on top to slip off. Obviously, random stone is unforgiving in these circumstances, and often the choice of suitable material is limited. As a result, any slope must be directed towards the inside of the structure, or should follow the wall's line. The width of the entire foundation is important, too: this has to be somewhere around 15–20in (38–50cm) from front to back.

Setting up the Batter Rods and String-lines

Before going any further you should set up the batter rods and string-lines. The two rods are hammered into the ground at each end of the construction site, 15–20in away from the earth bank. Next, tie the string to either one of the rods, 5in (12cm) above ground level, then take it to the opposite end. After threading the string around the next rod, pull it taught, then attach the line-level in the middle. With the string still tight, another person can watch the level's bubble, giving instructions to raise or lower the line. As soon as the string is level, tie it off. Now fix a second string-line on to the top of both rods, level it, and tie it off.

To create the batter, slightly push the rods towards the wall, around 2–3in (5–8cm). Standing at one end, look down the string-lines, ensuring the rods have a symmetrical lean. You can tell if they are even by checking the top and bottom strings: if the two are running parallel, then the batter is fine.

The aesthetic look of the front of the foundation is not an issue, as these stones will eventually be hidden from view; so if you have to turn a stone over for the sake of a wide base and the face then looks ugly, it doesn't matter. The stone must be substantial, as explained earlier: consider that whatever is laid as a foundation will have to support at least half of a tonne of material per metre. And in the case of a two-skinned wall, the burden is doubled.

Laying the End-Stones

With any walling course – and the foundation is no exception – it should always start from one end, then continue down the line of the wall until the course is complete. You should, however, lay the end-stones first and build between them. Wall ends (sometimes called 'cheek ends'), although they are tied into the body of a wall, can best be described as independent, free-standing pillars that act like book-ends for the face-stone, hearting and pinning. Like coping, their role is to seal the material that is otherwise exposed to the outside world, protecting the wall from animal, rain, frost and human damage. The stones you will be looking for should, if possible, be square-like and able to rest on a course with little or no pinning.

There are two types of end-stone: 'through-stones' (or 'throughs') and 'runners'. A through-stone literally travels through the wall, from front to back. On a double-skinned wall these stones bind the two faces together. Runners are long stones that 'run' down the length of a course. They normally come in pairs and are laid side by side. There is no fixed rule that states what style of end-stone you use to start a foundation course; you can lay a through-stone or a pair of runners. However, these first stones will dictate the pattern for the remainder of the wall end. If, for example, you lay a pair of runners, you must then use a through-stone to bind them together. After the second course is built, another pair of runners ties the 'through' underneath to the bulk of the wall. The alternating pattern continues until the dry-stone feature reaches full height.

Having laid the first end-stones at both ends, align their faces with the string-line, then check their stability by standing on them. If little or no adverse movement can be detected, the rest of the foundation course can be laid. Align the faces of these stones to the string. Where possible, lay them with their length pointing towards the earth bank.

When this course is complete, fill all the spaces between the stones and bank with hearting. The bulk of this hearting must be no smaller than your fist and filled to the same level as the top of the foundations, no higher. Check the foundations' stability by walking up and down the stones – though please note that when the second course of face-stone is laid, standing on the wall will cause a collapse.

Laying Face-Stones

First choose an end to start from, and then begin. Finding the right face-stone for any given section of wall is just as much of a skill as the act of walling itself. Working with random stone can appear daunting to begin with, especially if you are expected to create a professional-looking example of countryside furniture. To the untrained eye, natural stone seems to lack any of the building qualities one would expect to find in a house brick. Bricks are smooth, flat and easily stacked; stone is oddly shaped with numerous bumps and indents, features that produce a wobble. To the lay person this is part of the enigma, but if you were to look at a haphazard pile of rock, around 95 per cent of it could actually build a stable boundary or retaining wall. A dry-stone waller can recognize the shape and form of each rock, and is able to relate it to strong walling courses.

All experienced wallers, when searching for stone to lay, run a series of questions through their mind: Does the stone have a vertical side that can face out from the wall? Most stones, regardless of their shape, will come with a suitable face. Will I be able to build a course on top of it? Will it leave enough space for the stone that has to be laid on the other side? That last question only relates to double-skinned boundary walls, as a stone that spans a retaining wall's width is ideal.

Building up the Courses

Before starting the second course, raise the lower string-line 5in (13cm) above the foundation stones. Remember that even this layer will have to sustain a heavy load, and therefore choose the larger face-stones from your selection. Like the bottom course, face-stones are laid with their larger surface areas on the wall. You should also strive to set their lengths running towards the earth bank for stability.

Having found the perfect stone, gently lower it on to the course, abutting it to the end-stone, then manoeuvre its face until it is parallel with the string-line. You will notice the stone isn't secure by the fact it will probably wobble when light force is applied. The following test and technique will counter the problem: ensuring the stone remains in position, apply down-ward pressure on the front surface with your hand, and then rock it from side to side and backwards and forwards. Do this until the stone jams against the course below. Insert small, wedge-shaped pinning into the gaps generated by the test, but only do this from behind. If you were to insert pinning into the front of the wall, it would eventually fall out. Build the remainder of the course to the opposite end-stone, then begin the second layer of face-stone.

The subsequent courses of face-stone are laid in the same fashion, placing the stone lengthways into the wall and allowing it to rest on the hearting below. The higher you go, the smaller the face-stones should be; thus it is essential that each course is tied in securely by creating a bond with the material behind. A further stabilizing attribute is the addition of a 'through-band' halfway up the wall. This is a course of wall that is composed of through-stones, every 2–4ft (60cm–1.2m), abutted against normal face-stones.

The final layer of walling is the coping. On a retaining wall, coping is flat, spanning the entire structure and resting on the earth behind. A two-sided boundary wall's coping is laid edgeways, crossing both faces.

I must stress that this has only been a concise guide to dry-stone walling, serving to give you no more than a basic grounding. For your further information, *A Guide to Dry Stone Walling* (Crowood, 2001) describes the craft in greater detail.

CHAPTER 6

GABIONS

Gabions are retaining walls put together by loading large rectangular mesh baskets or cages with random walling stone. They are typically used to counter the effects of erosion on the side of rivers by creating permanent artificial banks. Although somewhat ugly in appearance, gabions are a highly effective alternative to stone retaining walls in rivers with a fast-flowing, eroding current. The baskets come in many styles including nylon, plastic and polypropylene, but the stronger types are made of galvanized steel, making them perfect for rigorous outdoor conditions such as in the rebuilding of washed away river paths. Gabions can be installed following the same construction principle as that of a dry-stone

galvanized steel
basket packed
with walling stone

backfilled with
large hearting

construct all external
faces using the dry-
stone walling method

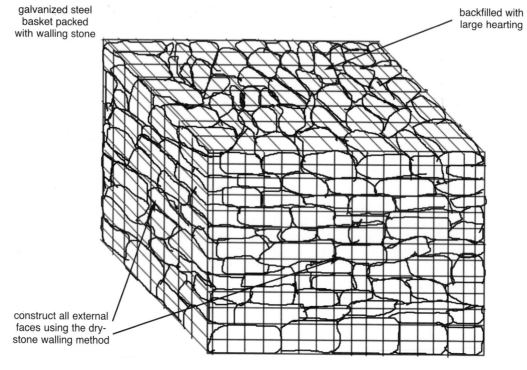

Repairing a riverbank – step 1.

wall, and require no specialist equipment to complete a project, only basic tools.

Using gabions in rivers instead of stone retaining walls will deliver numerous structural benefits. One problem with walls is 'scour', or the erosion of matter underneath the wall's foundation. Scour will eventually cause a collapse. Adding a layer of large rocks to form a 'toe' on the riverbed, in front of the revetment, can reduce scour – though even with this protection the wall's mortar can still be swept away in strong currents. Gabions, on the other hand, are tightly packed with stone and the surrounding cages hold the contents so securely that hardly any movement develops. With the addition of stone-toe protection, erosion is virtually eliminated.

Building Gabions

All river tasks are best carried out when the water current and level is at its lowest, probably during the summer months. The riverbed in front of the eroded bank must be levelled as much as possible in order to create a stable base. Gabion cages come 'flat-packed', to be unfolded on site.

Like a dry-stone wall, the building process begins from one end to the next. After joining the panels of the first basket with the heavy duty, key-ring-style connectors that are supplied with it, it can be lifted into place. The second basket is then unfolded and connected to the first, using the same fixings, and this continues until the eroded bank has been

join the gabions using the supplied connectors

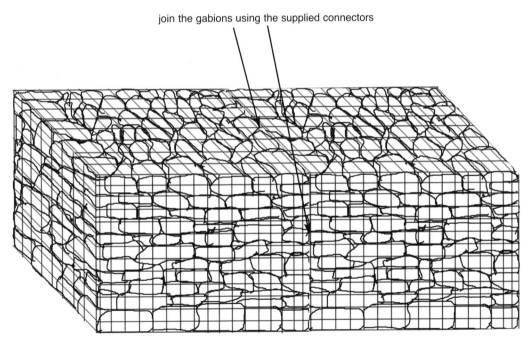

Repairing a riverbank – step 2.

completely faced. Do not, at this stage, attach the gabions' lids.

Loading the Stone

I have seen cages where the stone has just been tipped in with a mechanical loader, but filling them like this produces an uneven, unsightly look. I much prefer to construct the faces as I would a dry-stone wall, building it with interlocking courses, then carefully backfilling with hearting larger than the mesh gaps (*see* Chapter 5 for the walling technique). It does extend the time spent on the job, but it also yields a quality of appearance that Special Landscape Areas, national parks and other sensitive sites expect and demand.

It is important to thoroughly pack all the space inside the cages with stone larger than the mesh. If this isn't acted on correctly the river will soon drive the contents out and the steel will flex and deform. The perfect face-stone and hearting size is between 5–10in (12–25cm).

When all the gabions are full, the lids are attached using the supplied connectors.

Stone Toe Protection

You really only require a 'stone toe' where the revetment will be subjected to immense forces. Nevertheless, some form of scour barrier is required, as erosion will take place over time. The stone toe is a protective layer of relatively big rocks that originate from the gabions' base, spanning a width of around 4ft (1.2m) on the riverbed in front. The rocks are laid according to the direction of water flow. For example, on a river's 'swan neck' where the flow is towards the bank, toe-stones are laid end down, leaning with the gush.

Landscaping

Creating a sympathetic top or 'crown' is important for aesthetic image, as steel

3 gabions joined

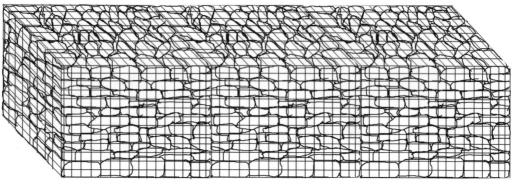

Repairing a riverbank – step 3.

if you need to stack gabions to build a higher bank, they should
be stepped with their back dug into the soil behind

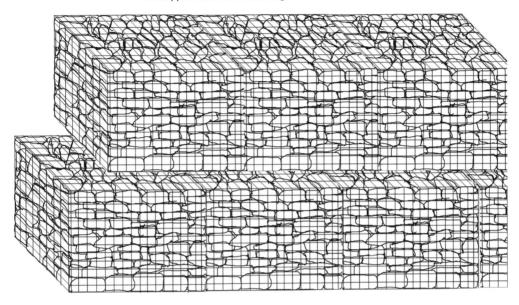

Stacking gabions.

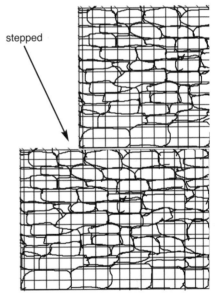

stepped

cages introduced into the rural idyll will stand out like the proverbial sore thumb. However, a wire basket packed with stone is not the ideal subsurface to initially fix the soil required to establish new flora, because rain will wash it off and walkers will take it away in the cleats of their boots. Fortunately there are commercial options in the form of pre-seeded matting. The matting is made of biodegradable 'coir' and seeded with wild, indigenous flora to suit most sensitive areas. The material is laid over a copious soil base, and then pinned down to hold the loam together. This has a secondary effect in that the coir will maintain the soil structure until the seed roots begin to bind it together. By the time flowers have matured, the matting begins to break down, eventually rotting down completely. Coir matting is also available on its own, allowing you to sow your own seed mixtures through the perforations. Its graze-resistant qualities ensure a barrier against hungry livestock.

CHAPTER 7

BUILDING WOODEN STEPS

Wooden steps should only be installed where there is no other way of dealing with an erosion problem on a slope. In many areas they will look out of place, especially in unspoiled upland regions. On busy walking routes, wear of the step surface and damage to timber supports and risers is a common factor in their high maintenance lifespan, making them a potentially expensive option. One must also consider the user. A long flight of stairs can be a daunting obstacle to the less able-bodied and to the elderly. Of all countryside furniture, wooden steps are the most awkward to build correctly.

Straight lines are another undesirable consequence of steps; they look out of place in an undulating terrain. One suggestion is that long passages of steps should be toned down by adding the occasional bend, and this is an excellent idea, and does break the monotony of climbing. Technically, you will only be able to apply them to a public right of way if the path itself bends and curves; otherwise you will be building off the definitive line. You can, if the angle of the slope allows, alternate steps with ramps, making the ascent less tiring for walkers – in fact, this is standard practice.

So, what are the conditions that dictate the need for steps? Some projects are undertaken as a result of requests from local people, via their Community Councils who then pass it on to a local authority's Highways Department or Countryside Service. The majority of projects arising from these requests tend to be small-scale constructions, usually on dog-walking routes similar to the first project chosen for this chapter. Major step construction really is a last resort solution, and is only considered if the slope has suffered extreme erosion and poses a danger to walkers where the route has become muddy, deeply rutted and slippery. The latter will only occur on the busy routes. The last thing you want to see in the countryside, where around 70 per cent of public footpaths traverse a hill, is a landscape full of wooden staircases.

There are alternative solutions, some of which are discussed in this book. A stone-pitched track, for instance, would suffice on inclines between 15 and 20 degrees. The same slope could accommodate a minimum number of steps as part of a quality surfaced path. Urban parks have to consider people with physical disabilities, as do country parks. For this reason alone, access wherever possible has to be sympathetic for all path-user groups.

I have included this 'step' chapter because wooden step building is an integral part of countryside work. Personally, I would much rather build them out of native stone in sympathy with the local area. There are occasions, though, when timber is the only solution.

Recommended Materials

The height of the riser should be no more than 8in (20cm), with a length of no less than 2ft (60cm) and a thickness of 2in (5cm); a 6in (15cm) rise is much more comfortable to climb and the most common, mainly because commercially purchased, wooden board comes in a standard 6in width. Wooden steps are constructed very much like a revetment, with support posts called 'stobs' driven into the ground and risers attached behind. Round fencing stakes offer the strongest solution, as they tend not to snap when kicked by a walking boot. A more cost-effective answer is 2 × 2in square posts, but these will have to be driven in 18in (45cm) at least, otherwise they tend to move; 2in or 3.5in half-round stakes or rails are another option for risers. Most estate and countryside services store off-cuts left over from tasks; sawn into 2ft (60cm) lengths, they make ideal stobs.

Risers are affixed to the supports with 5in or 6in (13cm or 15cm) galvanized nails. Like the revetment boarding described earlier, these are driven

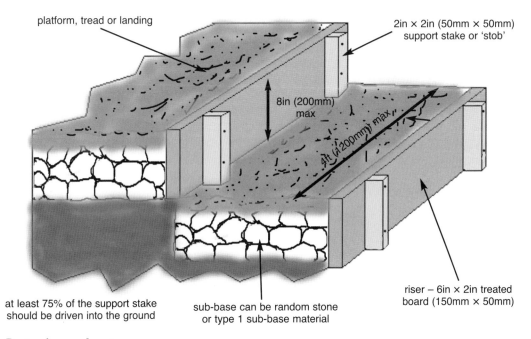

surface made of limestone dust with fines, not suitable for acid soil areas. an alternative is 'Hoggin', which is a clay-based top dressing.

platform, tread or landing

2in × 2in (50mm × 50mm) support stake or 'stob'

8in (200mm) max

4ft (1200mm) max

at least 75% of the support stake should be driven into the ground

sub-base can be random stone or type 1 sub-base material

riser – 6in × 2in treated board (150mm × 50mm)

Parts of a wooden step.

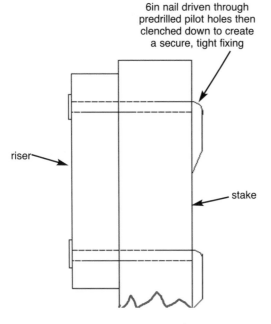

6in nail driven through
predrilled pilot holes then
clenched down to create
a secure, tight fixing

riser

stake

Fixing risers to support stakes.

This is what might happen if you secure the riser to the front of the support stakes. Steps may look less attractive when the stakes are visible but the structure will be more solid.

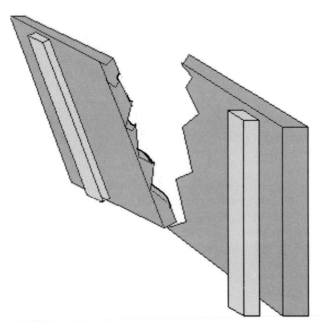

This could happen if the timber for the riser is too thin. A 2in-thick board is recommended.

through and clenched on the opposite side. The step platforms must be free draining and contain a subsurface of stone. An aggregate top surface, shaped to form a slight camber or slope to aid water run-off, is also recommended. There is hardly any point in repairing a muddy bank, then backfilling with just the excavated soil, because the steps will eventually become a worse quagmire. There is a safety consideration, too, because slipping on steps may result in severe injury to the user, whereas if they slide on a muddy bank, a pair of dirty trousers is all they'll probably walk away with.

Tool Requirements

- Spade.
- Mattock or pick.
- Crowbar.
- Fencing maul.
- Claw hammer.
- Tape measure.
- Handsaw.
- Manual drill or rechargeable drill.
- Spirit level.
- Tamper.
- Sledgehammer.
- Safety goggles.

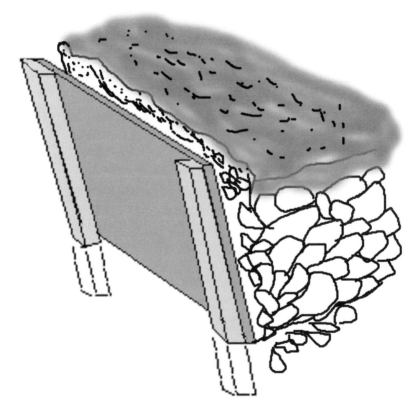

If support stakes are not driven in deep enough, the front of the step will soon give way, pushed forward by the pressure of path users' feet.

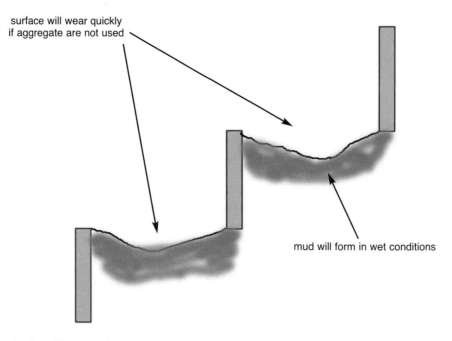

surface will wear quickly
if aggregate are not used

mud will form in wet conditions

Steps built without surfacing.

Method of Construction

When surveying a potential step project, you will need to estimate how many risers and platforms would make the easiest, safest ascent and descent. The preference should be on fewer risers and longer platforms, but the gradient will ultimately govern the outcome. On steep slopes expect to construct as many risers as there are platforms, whereas shallow inclines allow for fewer steps and more easygoing platforms. The best method for working out quantities is by measuring the height of the gradient, then dividing it by the riser height. Rather than estimating the slope, use a simple tool such as a clinometer, an instrument for measuring the angle of an object above or below the horizontal. It can be used for gauging the height of trees, or buildings,

or anything that stands vertical in the ground. To use a clinometer you look through an eyepiece on to an angle measuring scale and horizontal line; with your other eye you view the object you want to measure, the brow of a hill for example. When the horizontal line is aligned with the object, you read the scale.

Installing the First Riser

Having worked out the number of steps needed, the construction phase can begin. All step projects, without exception, start from the bottom of a hill. The first riser is the easiest to install, and normally all that's required is an accurate alignment of the riser to help align the two support stakes. First, excavate or level the soil, then lay the riser on the

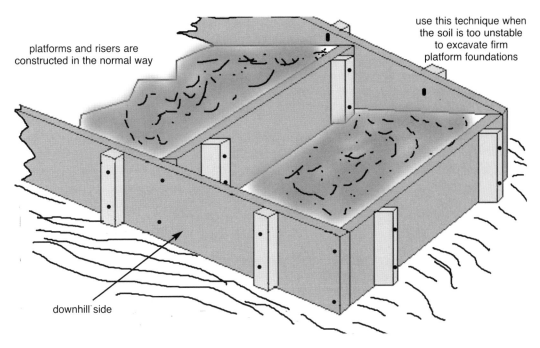

platforms and risers are
constructed in the normal way

use this technique when
the soil is too unstable
to excavate firm
platform foundations

downhill side

Installing a reveted staircase on loose soil structures.

ground. With a spirit level as a guide, adjust the timber by tapping lightly on the top edge with a fencing maul. Holding the riser in position, bore two postholes with the crowbar to a depth of at least 8in (20cm). Take one support stake, push it into one of the postholes, then drive it in with the maul. Repeat this for the second stake.

Nailing Up

The riser and stakes will require nail pilot holes. The fact that the nails are going to be clenched on the other side means that pilot holes can be driven through both sections of timber. After drilling two holes per stake, drive the nails in from the front and bend the points down, against the back of the riser. By now, the timbers should be sturdy

when pushed or pulled. If movement is detected other than the wood's natural flex, the step will not be strong enough to cope with the force of a user's downhill journey. Once you are satisfied with the feature's rigidity, saw the stakes level with the riser's top edge.

Dressing the Platform

The next phase is to load the stone sub-base up to within 2in (5cm) of the riser's top edge. Compact it with the sledgehammer or tamper. Before dressing the platform with aggregate, create a level platform for the second step. This may involve some grubbing work with the mattock or pick to break tree roots or remove stone. Try to excavate, to the level off the lower riser's top edge. Align and connect the second riser the same way as the previous one, then load the top dressing over the first platform and tamp down. The back of the platform should be slightly ramped towards the front, with a subtle sideways cross-fall to aid draining. The remaining steps are constructed using the same technique.

Larger Inclines

The last project highlighted the basic principles behind wooden step construction and was suitable for most small-scale tasks. Larger inclines and varying gradients pose more complex issues, including dealing with soil loss, water erosion and drainage. Depending on where the steps are to be sited, you may have to add a handrail or revetment boarding, or the route might change direction halfway up the hillside. The following guides will explain some basic customization techniques.

This next project was carried out by Denbighshire Countryside Service, and is a good example of how to recycle fencing materials left over from previous tasks.

The tools used to build the three steps described.

An eroded slope on a popular dog-walking route. In winter this became very slippery. Three simple steps were constructed using recycled fencing posts for risers.

Excavating a level foundation for the first platform.

Two sawn fencing stakes make one 6in (15cm) riser.

Using a crowbar to create a posthole for support stakes.

Driving in a support stake with a fencing maul.

Two stakes on the outside of the riser.

Pre-drilling for the nails.

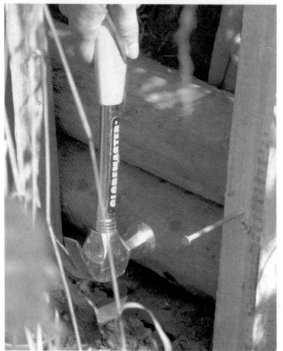

5in (13cm) nails connect the riser to the stake.

Saw a post level with the top edge of the riser.

Excavating the second platform.

The second riser is now ready for its support stakes.

Attaching the stakes to the third riser.

The finished job awaiting surfacing. One of the problems with mineral soil is buried stone. Sometimes, no matter how you try, stakes will glance off deep stone and skew.

Curves and Corners

Adding a curve to a flight of steps demands a gradual and subtle change of each riser's position in order to form a smooth, uniform bend. The skill isn't just in the knowledge of construction; it is knowing when a change of direction warrants a corner. A basic theorem with countryside stairways is to maintain a safe, roomy walking platform, and curves, by default, reduce the amount of platform you can stand on. Space is lost on the inside of the curve, for this end of the riser has to be moved forwards to produce the turn. Corners are not necessarily built on 90-degree angles; they should be located when the depth of tread becomes so small they are a hazard. The opinion here changes somewhat, but I feel if any part of the upper riser comes to within 3in (8cm) of the lower one, an area of the platform becomes too narrow, allowing room for only the ball of the foot on ascent and the heel on descent. One should consider installing a corner here.

Initiating a curve is simple. Assuming you have already built the stairway up to the point of turn, infill the platform's subsurface as described earlier. Align the riser in the standard way, then move the end on to the inside of the bend, 2–4in (5–10cm) towards the lower step. Holding that position, create postholes, drive in support stakes, and affix the wooden board, as described earlier. You will now be left with a moderately wedge-shaped platform. After excavating the upper platform and loading it with a rock subbase, align the next riser until it is parallel with the lower one. Now move the end,

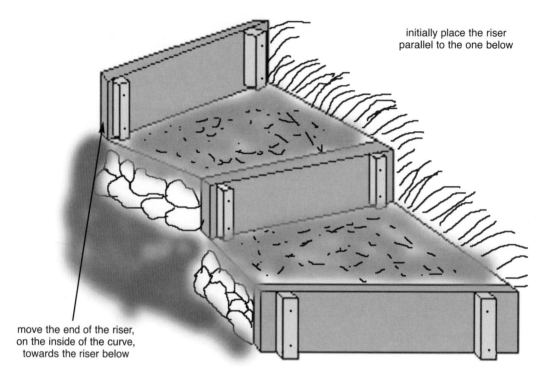

initially place the riser parallel to the one below

move the end of the riser, on the inside of the curve, towards the riser below

Making a curved stairway.

on the inside of the curve, as described for the first.

Lastly, connect the riser to its support stakes. After around four steps have been constructed in this manner, the bend will begin to take shape; how far you actually adjust the risers will depend on how sharp it is. If at any time the end of the board comes to within 3in (8cm) of the lower riser, consider creating a corner.

Creating a Corner

Installing a corner involves more work and materials. Changing direction on a slope at this acute angle will mean that the relationship of the steps to the hill has changed. On one side the ground rises, on the other it falls away, and the installation will have to be sturdy enough to carry the foundation and the top surface, as well as path users.

A project like this is, in effect, an amalgamation of the methods employed on the revetment boarding described in Chapter 4, and the steps already discussed in this chapter. The steps and the revetments on the uphill side will only necessitate the use of 2in × 2in stakes, but on the downhill part you will almost certainly have to drive in 3in (8cm) round posts: any lesser diameter may only create a hazard. The revetment boarding does not have to be the length depicted in Chapter 4, it need only be the length of the corner's platform, and the depth of drop on the downhill side will dictate the quantity required to bring the step up to height. The follow-

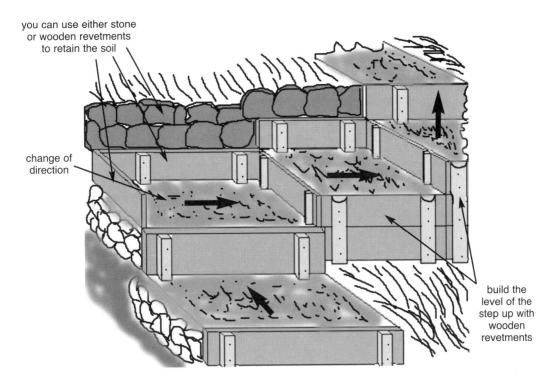

you can use either stone or wooden revetments to retain the soil

change of direction

build the level of the step up with wooden revetments

Adding corners.

ing diagram shows an example of what is required.

Building Handrails

Handrails, I feel, should only be instated where they are most effective. They are obtrusive and out of character with a track winding its way up pleasant hillside. In some instances, where safe travel is essential, it is necessary to add some style of support for the safety of path users. On routes climbing a fairly sheer cliff and on very steep stairways, users will benefit from the security and help of a handrail. A handrail, countryside fashion, is basically built like a post-and-rail fence in that a fencing stake is driven in

every 6ft (1.4m), and 12ft (3.6m) rails are attached (*see* my book *A Guide to Stock Fencing* (Crowood, 2002) for details).

Here, a basic method for building a handrail is described that would suit most situations.

Materials Required

The quantity of wood needed will depend on the length of your path or stairway. In the next example, the flight of steps covers a distance of 24ft (6.4m), and the material requirement will be as follows:

- 2 × 12ft (3.6m) machined, half-round rails; these will be used for the top handrails. Half rounds are more suitable than square rails for three

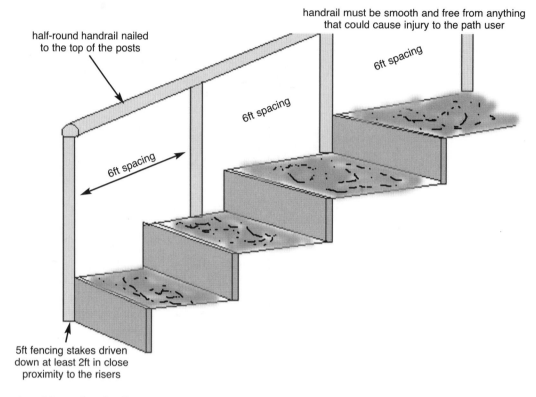

handrail must be smooth and free from anything
that could cause injury to the path user

half-round handrail nailed
to the top of the posts

6ft spacing

6ft spacing

6ft spacing

5ft fencing stakes driven
down at least 2ft in close
proximity to the risers

Attaching a handrail.

reasons: firstly, they tend to be smoother (having said that, some sanding and smoothing is usually recommended). Secondly, they have rounded tops, which allows for better grip. Lastly, they are stronger than square rails. Square rails, when subjected to pressure, may snap on wood knots; half rounds are more resistant to collision or weight damage. If stock proofing is an issue, the lower rails can be square. You could also staple on and strain a section of sheep netting instead. Netting is also convenient if you wish to affix some sort of path-user security, on the edge of steep slopes, for example. Cliff faces may demand the construction of steel rails.

- 5 × 5ft × 3in (1.5m × 7.5cm) machined round, pointed stakes; these will act as the rail supports. The half rounds are actually nailed to the top of the posts. Each rail must be propped by three supports. For two 12ft rails you are looking at one post at either end of the handrail, another where the two rails join, and a further two placed where the half rounds are at their weakest, that is between the first and middle support and the middle and last. This equates to one post every 6ft (1.4m).
- 5in galvanized nails.
- 4in galvanized nails, if square rail is to be attached as stock proofing.
- Fencing staples if sheep netting is going to be attached.

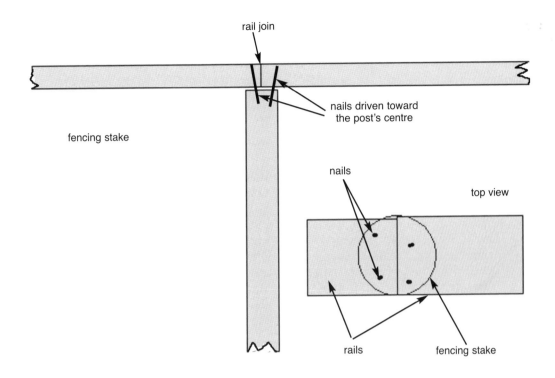

rail join

nails driven toward
the post's centre

fencing stake

nails

top view

rails

fencing stake

Attaching a handrail – 2.

Tool Requirements

- Crowbar.
- Fencing maul or post slammer.
- Hand drill or rechargeable drill, complete with suitable bits for creating nail pilot holes in the rail.
- Hand saw.
- Surform rasp or sander.
- Tape measure.
- Spirit level.
- String-line.

The following tools are only needed if attaching wire.

- Fencing pliers.
- Bar strainer or chain strainers.
- Wire cutters.

Method of Construction

Start by making a posthole adjacent with the bottom riser, using the crowbar. These support stakes have to be vertical and deep, therefore each posthole must be dug out to a good depth. Next, hammer in the first 5ft (1.5m) post, intermittently checking it with a spirit level, to a depth of at least 1.5ft, and 2ft (60cm) if it will go down that far. The next stake will be on the top of the flight, inserted as just described. It is worth noting that if any part of the stairway changes direction, the next post should be inserted there, and another if the direction alters again, and so on – straight runs are less complicated.

All of the posts will have to be set precisely, especially where the rails meet.

The space from each of the posts' centres is 6ft (1.8m). A tape measure could be used for distance marking, but in my experience not all '12ft' rails seem to be 12ft (3.6m) long. The most exact method is to lay the rails in a line, from bottom to top, making a template for the postholes.

After the lower and upper posts are firmed in, you should attach the string-line somewhere near the halfway point of the lower post, and then tie it on to the stake at the brow of the hill. For ease of post positioning, ensure the string is tensioned on the side facing the steps. With the string and rail template in place, drive in the third post where the two rails join. Take the crowbar and mark the ground adjacent to the join. Next, move the rails apart, then manoeuvre the bar until it is about 1in away from the string when held vertical. Make a posthole, and drive the stake in as described earlier.

The reason for marking the posthole a little distance from the string-line is that the crowbar's point represents the central point of a fencing stake, and not the edge. If you made a posthole with the bar touching the string, the stake, when knocked in, would push the string out of profile. Drive the third stake down, making sure it just brushes the string-line. The next part of the job concentrates on the two remaining support stakes; as stated earlier, these are hammered into the ground at 6ft (2m) spacing between the stakes now in situ.

A comfortable height for the handrail would be about 3.5ft (1m), and no less than 3ft (90cm). Before you can nail the rails on, you should saw the post tops to handrail height.

Securing the Handrail

Working from the bottom of the step line, take one rail and lift it on to the first three supports. Ensuring that one rail-end is flush with the outside edge of the lower post and the other just reaches the centre of the third, pre-drill two pilot holes through the rail at the bottom of the slope. Only penetrate the rail; not the post's top. For the moment, drive home one 5in (13cm) nail; it allows the rail to be adjusted more easily if needs be. Concentrating now on the third support post, create two more pilot holes in the rail-end and drive home two nails. Lastly, bore the holes for the second support and then affix the rail. Don't forget to insert the second nail on the first post. The

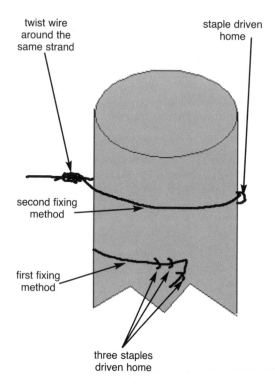

twist wire around the same strand

staple driven home

second fixing method

first fixing method

three staples driven home

Attaching stock wire.

following rail is attached using the same technique.

If you are attaching stock proofing or safety rails, these can be nailed on to the side of the supports. For containing stock, fasten them to the stock side (the side of the fence facing the pasture); for use as a safety barrier, secure them to the side facing the steps.

Securing Netting

If the handrail design calls for stock netting, proceed as follows. After removing the string-line, lift the roll of stock wire to the bottom support. Stand the roll on end ensuring that the smaller squares (not the larger ones) are closest to the ground. Stock netting is comprised of horizontal and vertical wire strands. The horizontal wires are used for tensioning, and run from one end of the roll to other; the vertical strands help produce the stock-proofing squares, which decrease in size. The smaller squares, at low level, are intended to prevent smaller creatures escaping, such as lambs.

If you are breaking into a new roll, find the ends of each horizontal wire (they will be turned into the coil). Using the pincer end of the fencing pliers, lever them out one by one. On reaching the last strand, be wary of the roll uncoiling quickly; on no account try to stop it. When the coil is stable, it is ready to be stapled to the first support. There are two ways you can do this: the first method just involves hammering three fencing staples over each horizontal strand and clenching the wire downwards. The second method involves threading each wire around the post, then twisting it a few times around the same strand. It doesn't matter which technique is used; what is important is to keep the whole roll upright. This is easily achieved by pushing the crowbar through the middle of the coil and into the ground.

Working with the first fixing method, pull out around 3ft (90cm) of netting, then place the bottom, horizontal wire against the post, leaving a gap of 2–3in (5–8cm) from the ground. Next, drive home a fencing staple until it grips the wire, making sure you leave at least 3–4in (8–10cm) of bare wire on the other side of the staple. Drive a second staple over the wire, leaving a 1in (2.5cm) gap between the two. With the fencing pliers or hammer, bend the remaining wire down 90 degrees or so, then secure to the post with a third staple. You may notice that the strand between the first and second staple bulges slightly: this is called a 'friction bulge', and shows that the wire is securely fixed, and will not slide through when tensioned. Attach the remaining strands using the same method. Please refer to the diagram for a description of the second wire-fixing technique.

With the end wires fixed, move the roll of netting up to the top of the steps, taking the roll 2ft to 3ft (60–90cm) past the last support stake. Before propping it up with the crowbar, take hold of the netting in both hands and pull it tight against the posts. Working on the last post, drive two staples over the top wire strand: for the time being, leave a small amount of clearance. Using a bar strainer, tension the wire as tight as you can. Whilst holding the strain, hammer the two staples home. Now cut the top wire, leaving roughly 2in (5cm) of bare strand. With the claw hammer, bend this bare strand down 90 degrees, and drive in the third staple. Now, repeat for the bottom wire strand. The reason that the top and bottom wires are tensioned first is because they are designed to hold a degree of high tension. They are, in fact, made of high tensile material, whereas the intermediate, horizontal strands are lower tensile, designed to be tensioned with a small tool such as fencing pliers. You can, however, tension them with the bar strainer.

The last job is to attach the wire to the remaining supports, only this time leave a small gap between fixing and timber to allow for expansion and contraction of the netting in hot and cold weather.

A completed flight of wooden steps built by staff at Ty-Mawr Country Park, Wrexham.

CHAPTER 8

BUILDING STONE STEPS AND LANDINGS

Stone steps and landings offer a better, more durable alternative than their wooden cousins. In uplands, where stone is easily available, this is the preferred style because they blend in with the natural bedrock of any given region. There are varying techniques associated with differing sizes of stone. Some steps are built using one or two large stones as riser and platform; others are built in the same fashion as a wet-stone wall. Stone sizes will largely depend on the availability of supply and on budget, but on high-profile and heavily walked routes most organizations prefer sizeable materials. This concurs with the adage: 'If it requires two people to manoeuvre a stone, it won't move when one person walks on it.'

I will describe two projects in this chapter that I hope will encompass most of the techniques you will probably ever need to know. The first is a mortared stone landing, complete with steps, in an area called Lady Clough within the Peak District National Park. It was a major volunteer task that went ahead in the late 1980s and took around five months to complete. There are two reasons I chose this one for the book: first, I had the pleasure of supervising a number of volunteer groups on the task; and second, the finished product is as strong today as it was almost twenty years ago. Admittedly I wasn't the only volunteers' supervisor to have put the work in: it was a joint team effort between everyone associated with the Peak National Park's conservation volunteers' programme. I won't give a graphic description of the entire job as this would take too long, but will just concentrate on the construction of two major features, a natural stone landing and step.

Materials

- Around 1 tonne per square metre of indigenous random stone. The quantity is only a guide and is an overestimate, for the simple reason that various sections of terrain used more stone than others on the route.
- Sand and cement.
- Sand and gravel mix for concrete.
- A substantial water supply.
- Plasticizer; a solution that creates viscosity in mixed mortar, enabling easy pointing of joins. For winter tasks you can use a solution that includes anti-freeze.

Tool Requirements

- Spade.
- Crowbar.
- Pick.
- Mattock.
- Shovel.
- Rubber maul for bedding in large stone.
- Lump hammer for bedding in smaller stone.
- Bucket, handy for storing mixed mortar, hearting stones and pinning.
- String-line.
- Pointing trowel.
- Wheelbarrow, for transporting materials around the site. Can be used as a receptacle for mixing sand and cement.
- Fuel-powered cement mixer. This is obviously the preferred cement-mixing tool.

Building a Stone Landing

As with all step-construction tasks, start from the bottom of the slope. This is more crucial when building in stone because the higher step must bridge the lower one. The first phase of the project is constructing the landing. It begins with excavating a base trench down to a firm subsoil structure in order to sustain the heavy stone structure that is going to be laid on top. Digging to a depth of around 6in (15cm) usually suffices, but on waterlogged soils you may have to go deeper. Having dug the trench, the base should be inspected for soft areas; tamping in medium- to small-sized rocks can firm these.

The next job is to prepare a small foundation trench around the inside edge of all four foundation sides. The trench here does not have to be deep; it is merely a holding receptacle for the concrete used to set the base stones. An excavation of around 3in (8cm) deep and 5in (13cm) wide would normally be adequate. Once these foundations are complete, concrete containing one part cement, four parts sand and gravel can be shovelled in and levelled with a trowel.

Now the wall foundations have been prepared, the first walling stones can be laid. These are placed on a bed of mortar incorporating one part cement, three parts sand and an addition of anti-freeze/plasticizer solution. Trowel a 2in (5cm) layer of mortar on to the concrete foundation, enough to cover an area suitable for three stones (though the amount will depend on stone size). The walling method is exactly as described in Chapter 5; to briefly recap, lay the stones with their lengths set towards the centre of the trench, and insert pinning underneath to stop movement.

Finding the Right Stone

Firstly, always have a full bucket of pinning, and place it at arm's length from the immediate construction area. Next, search for a stone with decent length; ideally it should have a smooth top and underside, but it will more than likely turn out to be an odd shape. If that's the case, turn the smoother side uppermost and bed the stone into the mortar, with its face touching the side of the trench. Taking the rubber mallet, gently tap it downwards until the mortar starts to ooze out from all sides. The top of the stone needs to be level for the next course. If it is seems to be sloping into the trench, carefully lift it and insert pinning from behind, then pack it with as much small stone as you can. Using the trowel, skim the 'oozed-out' mortar up all sides of the stone, gently forcing it in and around the pinning.

Next, trowel a quantity of fresh mortar on to the side of the stone in preparation for the next stone. Lay a second stone, of similar height, on the foundation and abut to the first, then bed it down with the rubber mallet. You may have to brace the first stone with your free hand in case it becomes misaligned. Now place a third stone against the second, working as before. Shovel in a generous pile of mortar at the back. With the trowel, skim it to form a slope at the back of the stones. Continue laying stone like this until the wall's foundation is complete.

There is a reason why I suggested placing stones in threes. It is not a good idea to use too much mortar on the wall at one time, lest it dries out in hot weather or becomes waterlogged in damp conditions. Keeping the mortar in good condition is essential for the best possible bond.

You should now be left with a course of walling surrounding the inside of the landing foundation. Fill this cavity with hearting to the same level as the top surface of the walling stones. Working from the front of the feature, trowel a 2in (5cm) layer of mortar over one corner. You will now need to search for a stone that can bridge at least one of the joins on either side of the angle. Ideally its shape should be square, but if that can't be found, source one with two straight faces. Lay this stone gently on the mortar. Then, with a long spirit level resting on the corner stone, and spanning the *width* of the landing, tap the corner down until the level's bubble just touches or passes the 'level guide' furthest from the wall edge.

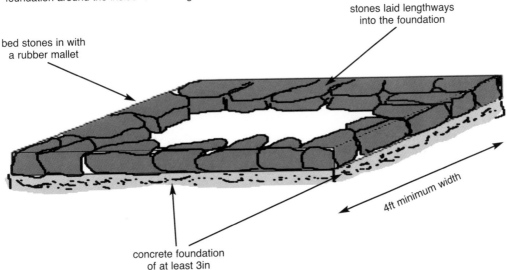

after excavating the landing's foundation, dig a further foundation around the inside for bedding in the stone

stones laid lengthways into the foundation

bed stones in with a rubber mallet

4ft minimum width

concrete foundation of at least 3in

Building stone steps and landings – step 1.

angled cemented skim around
the back of the stones

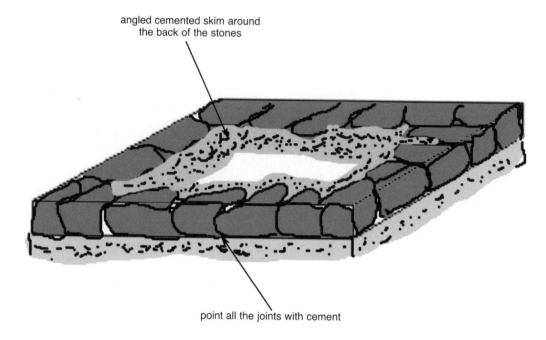

point all the joints with cement

Building stone steps and landings – step 2.

fill the centre of the landing with hearting, but
only to the level of the top of the walling stone

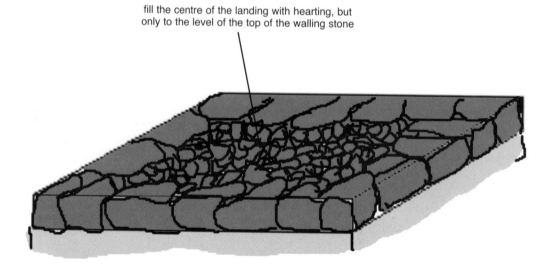

Building stone steps and landings – step 3.

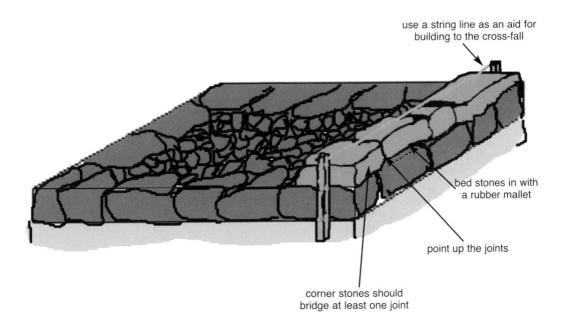

use a string line as an aid for building to the cross-fall

bed stones in with a rubber mallet

point up the joints

corner stones should bridge at least one joint

Building stone steps and landings – step 4.

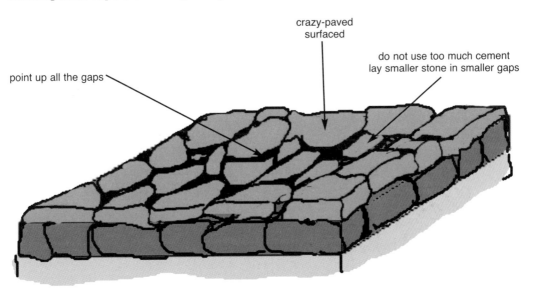

crazy-paved surfaced

do not use too much cement lay smaller stone in smaller gaps

point up all the gaps

wash off excess cement with a soft brush and clean water

Building stone steps and landings – step 5.

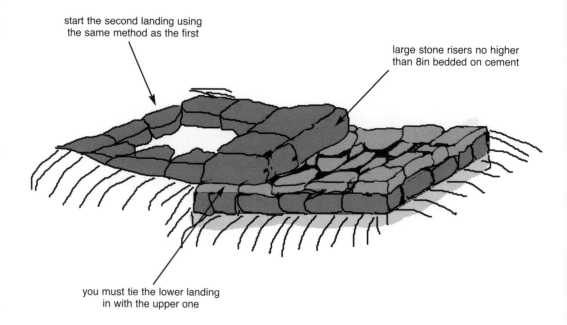

start the second landing using
the same method as the first

large stone risers no higher
than 8in bedded on cement

you must tie the lower landing
in with the upper one

Building stone steps and landings – step 6.

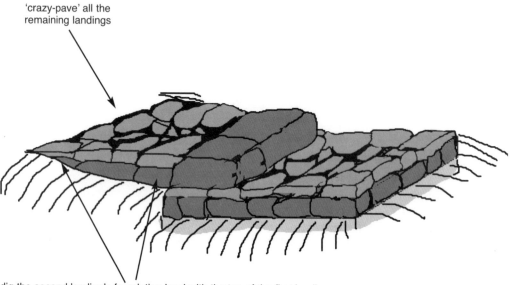

'crazy-pave' all the
remaining landings

dig the second landing's foundation level with the top of the first landing
excavate back until the internal, earth walls reach a height of 6–8in

Building stone steps and landings – step 7.

large tread can be pinned with large stone from behind. you may need to use a crowbar to lift the back of the tread before inserting pinners.

if you have to build the riser using a number of stone courses, choose the largest flattest material ensure that you bridge all joints

the steeper the ground, the smaller the landing

Building stone steps and landings – step 8.

This helps to create a slight cross-fall for water run-off. If the landing runs parallel to the gradient, the cross-fall must be directed towards the downhill side.

Building Up the Rows

You can now use this cross-fall as a guide for the rest of the landing. First you will have to set up a string-line. Carefully hammer in a stake close to the new corner stone, and then do the same at the opposite end. Take the string-line and tie it to the stake nearest the corner, ensuring a clearance of around 1.5in (4cm) from the stone's top surface. Next, stretch the line to the next stake and move the string (up or down) until it is equal with the cross-fall. Lastly, tie it off. You can now lay the remainder of the row using this line as a guide.

It would be helpful if all the material were identical in size and thickness, but random stone isn't like that. For some stone you may need to use slightly more mortar to bring the landing to an equal height. Continue building in rows, moving the stakes and string after each completion. Due to the nature of random material you will find that the stone will go down in 'crazy-paving' fashion. Try to abut the edges of each stone as close as you can to the neighbouring one.

It is best to begin each crazy paving row by laying the end stones on the edges first. This will ensure the maximum coverage of material over these weaker points. Not all joins will be the same. Within the larger joins, bed in smaller material, tamping it down to the same level. Finish the landing by filling all the joins with mortar, then trowelling them flush with the walking surface.

The last task is to wash down the entire section with clean water and a soft brush. Rather than just throw water over the feature, dip the brush and gently scrub it. Further cleaning can take place when the mortar has hardened, probably during the second day's work.

Building a Step

The next phase of the project adds a step to the back of the ramp. First, excavate another landing foundation, digging its base to the same level as the walkway below. Its total length will be dictated by the hill's gradient: you will require less length on steeper slopes, and vice versa. An easy guide to work with is the depth of the landing's earth walls; they must be

between 6in (15cm) and 8in (20cm) deep. When that depth has been reached, building can begin.

The step treads have a dual role. Apart from being the mechanism by which you climb the hill, they also serve to bond the lower landing with the upper one. This being the case, lay the tread stones 6–12in (15–30cm) across the lower platform, embedded in a substantial seat of mortar. As a rule the treads will be the largest stones of your selection, but they may have to be laid in a number of courses to reach the desired height. It is better to show this method in pictorial format, so please refer to the project's diagrams for a graphic description. The remainder of the landing follows the method as described for the lower one.

The following set of photographs shows some more interesting designs based on the techniques just described.

A section of the Lady Clough steps in 2005.

An example of a flight of steep stone steps.

*Stone steps leading up to an access gate –
work carried out by Peak National Park
Authority conservation volunteers.*

A fine example of a cemented stone riser and platform – work carried out by Peak National Park Authority conservation volunteers.

A natural stone landing – work carried out by Peak National Park Authority conservation volunteers.

Volunteers install a limestone riser at Monsal Head in the Peak District.

CHAPTER 9

WOODEN STILES

A stock-proof wooden step-over stile consists of, first, two large 7ft (2.1m) uprights, inserted 2.5–3ft (75–90cm) into the ground. These posts are generally set 1yd (1m) apart from each other, leaving enough room for an adult to step over safely. For stock proofing, a 12ft (3.6m) fencing rail is sawn into four equal lengths and nailed across the uprights to create a ladder effect or frame.

For comfortable access two steps, or treads, should be inserted through the frame, one between the first and second rail (the low tread) and another between the second and third rail (the higher tread). The two treads will need to rest on a further four uprights (two on each side of the frame). The treads can run parallel with each other, when they are generally known as off-set, or they can be constructed so that the lowest step crosses underneath the high one. Both methods are acceptable.

Tool Requirements

- Spade.
- Crowbar.
- Tamper (or fencing stake).
- Claw hammer.
- Long spirit level (or post leveller).
- Wire cutters (if the stile is part of a netted stock fence).
- Fencing pliers.
- Hand saw.
- Tape measure.

Material Requirements

- 2 × 7ft × 3in × 4in (2.1m × 7cm × 10cm) posts (main stile uprights).
- 2 × 4ft × 3in × 4in (1.2m × 7cm × 10cm) posts (higher tread uprights).
- 2 × 3ft × 3in × 4in (90cm × 7cm × 10cm) posts (lower tread uprights).
- 1 × 6ft × 5in × 1.5in (1.8m × 12cm × 3.8cm) boards (to be sawn in half for two stile treads).
- 1 × 12ft × 3in × 1.5in (3.6m × 7cm × 3.8cm) rail for stock-proofing.
- A quantity of 3in (7cm) nails for the rails, and 5in (12cm) nails for the treads.

Building the Stile

If the stile is to be incorporated into a new fence line, then the main stile uprights should be inserted as part of the fencing-stake phase. There are two important reasons for this. Firstly, if it is a public right of way, then from the onset you are making an attempt to keep the path open, which should satisfy the local authority or anyone who may wish to

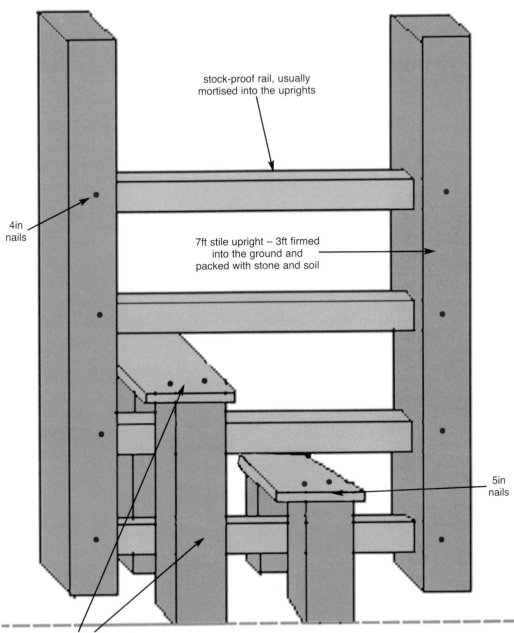

stock-proof rail, usually
mortised into the uprights

4in
nails

7ft stile upright – 3ft firmed
into the ground and
packed with stone and soil

5in
nails

stile treads and tread uprights
tread uprights inserted 2.5–3ft
into the ground and packed
with stone and soil

A standard stock-proof wooden step-over stile.

exercise their right to file a complaint. It is impossible at this stage to incorporate the treads because it will impede the travel of the netting, nevertheless it is a good idea to attach the rails so at least the main frame is in position. This will offer some form of passage for members of the public when the netting has been put on, which, by default, will be obstructing the path. The treads, however, should be set in place as soon as the stock-wiring phase is complete.

The main stile uprights can be inserted in exactly the same fashion as described in Chapter 3, checking the levels and firming them up against the string-line with stone and compacted soil. To achieve an accurate spacing, use one of the sawn fencing-rail cross-pieces.

As soon as the wire has been tensioned and stapled on, the tread section can be constructed. Start by excavating two trenches 2ft (60cm) in length, one on each side of the frame. The depth of the trenches should be the same as the main stile uprights. When firming up the tread uprights it is essential, for user safety, to make sure they are level, and that each opposing upright is of exactly the same height. The vertical strands of two small sections of netting will then need to be cut to allow the tread timbers through. As a precaution, before cutting the wire, staple it to the stile as if this were a strainer post (described in Chapter 3). Then push the treads through the netting so they rest on the uprights on each side of the fence. Use 5in (12cm) nails to secure them on, nailing two through each tread end. For safety, saw off the corners on each tread as they could be a possible cause of injury to a user whilst climbing over.

With the stile now in position, lawful public access can be maintained. When attaching the fence's top wire(s) do not run it across the frame. Cut the wire, tension it with either a bar strainer or fencing pliers (chain strainers may be too powerful for this section), and staple it to the first upright; then continue afresh with the second upright. If you are using barbed wire, the sharp points should be stripped off for a length of at least 1ft (30cm) each side of the stile uprights.

Adding a Stile to an Existing Fence

When creating access over an existing fence line it is vitally important that the wire remains intact. Existing tension should be maintained at all times for it to remain a viable stock-proof structure, and the holes for the main stile uprights will have to be excavated with the netting in position. This is not as difficult as it sounds, however, and it does, in fact, aid the uprights' final positioning.

CHAPTER 10

STONE STILES

To construct a stone step-over stile, at least two through-stones of about 3ft (90cm) in length will have to be inserted through the wall in order to create a small flight of steps or treads on each side. To enable comfortable, safe passage over the wall, each step will need to protrude at least 12in (30cm) from both faces of the wall.

Stone of a suitable size can be purchased from a quarry, but this could prove expensive on a limited budget. In the Peak District National Park most stone step-over stiles are built using concrete kerbstones. This is because around 80 per cent of the footpaths lead over dry-stone walls, and implementing a strategy with natural stone would not be cost effective. Another reason is that the material within the southern limestone area is not long enough to create a safe passage over a wall. The preferred option, of course, is to use natural stone when it is available, but kerbstones are fairly inexpensive and can be purchased from most large builders' merchants.

Some regions do have a strict policy on using natural stone, but it is usually where the local rock lends itself to the ideal size. Slate is perfect for this, as it can be split from the bedrock in large chunks.

To add a stone step-over stile, part of the wall will need to be taken down in the shape of a reversed apex. Start by removing a 6–8ft (1.8–2.4m) length of coping, and place the stones on one side. Look at both faces of the wall to see how the face-stones bridge the joins, and work out how best the stone can be removed to form steps on each edge. Take the wall down one course at a time, making sure that each step is secured.

If the wall is strong it will only need to be taken down to within two courses of the foundation. If, on the other hand, the stone within the structure is badly weathered, it should be removed down to the foundation stones.

Building in the Treads

The tops of the treads should be no more than 12in (30cm) apart, otherwise traversing the wall could be difficult. The first tread can usually be placed on top of the first course, and once in position it can be manoeuvred so its point of balance is directly over the centre of the wall. Check its horizontal path with a spirit level, and adjust as necessary by adding small face-stones underneath. For added strength and safety, some local authorities bed the treads and the surrounding

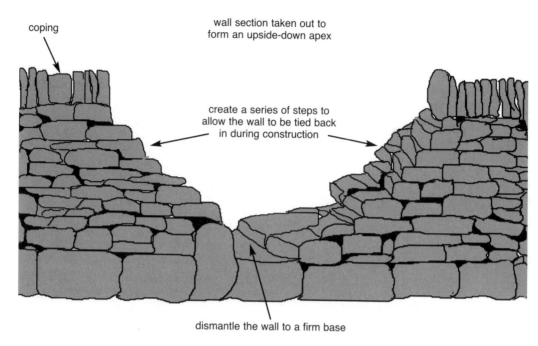

coping

wall section taken out to
form an upside-down apex

create a series of steps to
allow the wall to be tied back
in during construction

dismantle the wall to a firm base

Building a stone stile – step 1.

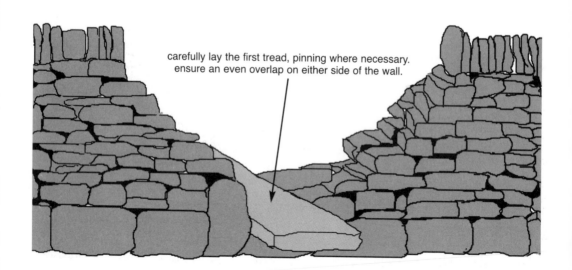

carefully lay the first tread, pinning where necessary.
ensure an even overlap on either side of the wall.

Building a stone stile – step 2.

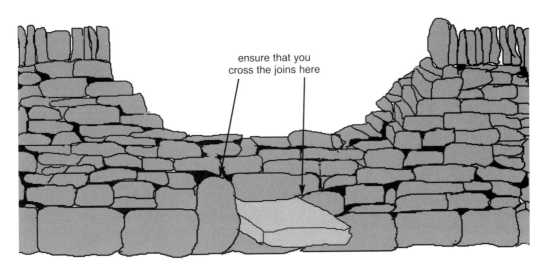

ensure that you
cross the joins here

build the next few courses, tying the face stone into the main wall

Building a stone stile – step 3.

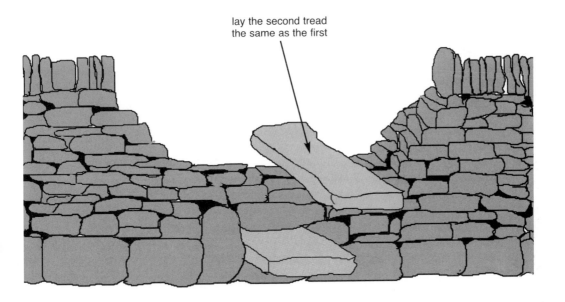

lay the second tread
the same as the first

Building a stone stile – step 4.

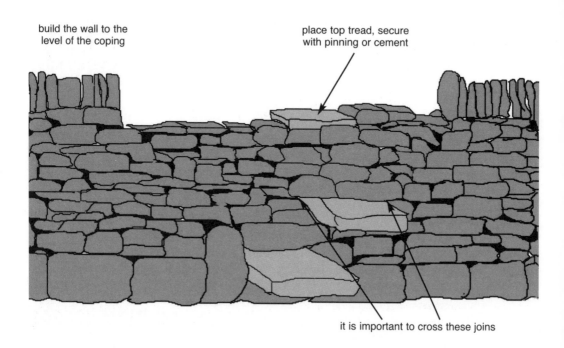

build the wall to the
level of the coping

place top tread, secure
with pinning or cement

it is important to cross these joins

Building a stone stile – step 5.

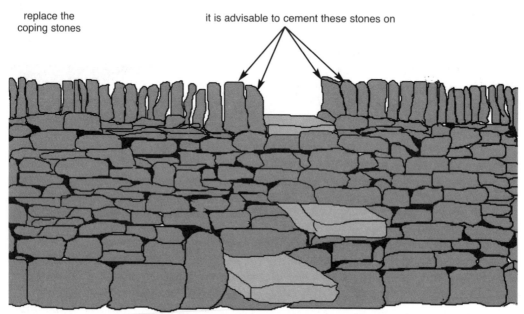

replace the
coping stones

it is advisable to cement these stones on

if the wall is higher, three treads or a launcher stone can be used

Building a stone stile – step 6.

An example of a stone step-over stile using recycled curbstones for treads.

stones in mortar. Although not in keeping with the philosophies of dry-stone walling, this is an acceptable compromise in situations where the safety of the public has to be taken into account. Colouring solutions can be added to the mortar to help it blend with the local stone, but in most cases they are not used. Add three parts sand to one part cement to form a strong solution.

Build up any gaps at the sides of the tread, then place a course of stone on top, bridging the joins of the tread and the wall on each side of the gap. Fill the wall's centre with hearting, and lay a further course of stone, adding mortar if required. Place further courses until the second tread can be inserted (remembering the tops of the two treads should be no more than 12in (30cm) apart). Secure this tread like the first, and then build the wall up to the top course of face-stone.

The actual crossing point of the stile will need to be directly above the second tread, leaving a 12–15in (30–40cm) gap in the coping to allow safe passage for the user. On most stiles this part of the structure is strengthened by a flat coping-stone, spanning the width of the wall and binding the two faces together. If one cannot be found, employ a mortared, crazy-paving arrangement.

Replace the coping stones using the method described in Chapter 4, leaving a 12–15in (30–40cm) gap above the second tread. Most walkers, when climbing a stile, will pull themselves up by holding on to the coping. With this in mind, each of the three coping-stones on each side of the crossing point should be bedded in mortar and pointed up in between.

On walls higher than 4ft 6in (1.3m) it is advisable to use three treads instead of two, for safe passage over the wall. If a three-treaded stile is built on a public footpath, or any public area, it is a health and safety requirement to place the treads at equal intervals apart. Where the ground is higher on one side, a 'launcher stone' can be bedded into the ground on the lowest side as a first tread. Squeeze stiles are only effective in enclo-sures containing large livestock and, in some cases, adult ewes, or in areas where stock proofing is not a priority. They are somewhat inadequate as a barrier for an inquisitive lamb or a goat bent on escape. This type of stile is rarely built nowadays, with most work carried out on the repair of existing ones. Where a footpath runs over an existing wall, the preferred option is to add a stone step-over stile because they are a better stock-proof device and less labour-intensive to implement. A squeeze stile requires a wall to be dismantled to its foundations, and then the assembling of two strong wall ends.

Adding a squeeze stile during the construction phase of a new wall may be an alternative if the right-shaped stone treads cannot be found. The stile should consist of two strong wall ends of about 15in (40cm) apart (refer to the technique for building wall ends, described in Chapter 4). For added strength, the end stones can be mortared in, because this will stop livestock or walkers from disturbing the stone as they pass through. A more common alternative is to initially dig two large stone pillars into the ground at roughly the same height of the wall, then to build dry-stone wall ends against these. If this method is going to be used, make sure it is the stone pillars that are 15in (40cm) apart, and not the wall ends.

CHAPTER 11

DEALING WITH EROSION

Since the first national parks were inaugurated in the 1950s, visitor numbers to these areas of beauty have increased. More people today are spending leisure time in the 'great outdoors', either by taking gentle valley ambles or powering to the summits of mountains such as Snowdon. The government, via various media, advises us to take generous amounts of healthy exercise – and what better way, both spiritually and physically, than to use the British countryside as a vehicle for health. But like all good things, there has to be a down side, and whilst we are getting fitter, the landscape is literally suffering at our feet: footpath erosion is now as common as moorland heather.

There are, of course, other sources of erosion that have varying degrees of impact on the land: flooding rivers, air pollution, heavy rainfall and even farm animals. All these have a detrimental effect – but the single most devastating factor is a walker's tread. As each footfall touches the ground, a blade of flora is compacted, and if the plant can't recover before the next set of feet presses down, it will eventually die, and all that will be left is bare soil. If the damage is unrepaired before the rains soak the ground, this bare patch of earth becomes muddy.

The mud then clings to the soles of boots and is carted off. In fact, the problem got so much worse in the 1970s and 1980s that walking-boot manufacturers began to sell their footwear with landscape-friendly soles. This was in the aftermath of studies showing that the 'commando-style' cleated sole, common to most boots, was probably the biggest culprit for taking soil away.

Changing the style of footwear was one step to alleviating a problem that was quickly getting out of hand, but as visitor numbers further increased, so did the eroded flora. Honey-pot paths such as the start of the Pennine Way in Edale, Derbyshire, and routes to the summits of popular high ground such as Snowdon and Scafel Pike were becoming terribly damaged, and the paths crossing the hillsides were increasingly becoming as wide as motorways, huge, man-made scars that could be seen from miles away.

How does a path turn into a broad, ugly eyesore? The answer is simple. People do not like walking through mud, and they avoid it by walking on the drier, grassy areas on each side. As these lush sections suffer increasing wear, new mud forms, and so the path widens. Imagine this scenario occurring over one thousand times in a single day. Perhaps the most pronounced example of this problem took place in Grindsbrook Meadows, Edale. Grindsbrook Meadows is the celebrated start of Britain's first long-distance foot-path, the Pennine Way. It is also the beginning of a major ascent to Kinder Scout, a peat and heather plateau made famous by the Kinder Trespass in 1932. These two factors have made Kinder one of the most visited rural sites in the UK – and over the years this has taken its toll.

During my time with the Peak District National Park Authority, the small team I worked with conducted experimental repair work on the Pennine Way. Some projects were successful, and some failed; such is the nature of pilot ventures. On one section of the path we installed large, polystyrene blocks inside a trench, on top of a hardcore sub-base. This was topped with black basalt to blend with the sur-rounding peat. The finished section looked professional and the surface was easy to walk on – easy, that is, until it rained. And then the polystyrene did the one thing it is good at, which is floating, and as the moorland water table rose (normal for winter), so did the blocks. Mercifully they didn't float away, thanks to the experimental means of keeping them securely in place at each end. It was, nonetheless, a problem for the unsuspecting hiker who, after enjoying a firm surface, suddenly found himself

Grindsbrook Meadows in Edale – extensive visitor pressure caused this huge scar (reproduced with permission from Mike Rhodes, Peak District National Park).

standing on a path that rippled like water with every step.

Although my personal input was miniscule compared with the strategies that followed, these successful failures played their part in gaining the award-winning projects implemented today. Entire stretches of eroded upland path have been restored by highly skilled craftspeople, working on mountainous terrains, sometimes in the foulest weather conditions Britain can throw at them. On occasions their work sites are inaccessible to all but the walker, and helicopters have to be commissioned to airlift in tools and materials. It is now a common occurrence to see one of these aircraft hauling large bags of stone in and around mountain ranges, servicing teams working above 2,000ft (600m).

Stone Pitching

The trials that took place in the 1980s have led to a procedure of repair that is one of the oldest techniques of building a path: stone pitching, acknowledged as the most aesthetic, stable method for rectifying years of damage. The skill of stone pitching is on a par with dry-stone walling, and the craftspeople who operate in and around Britain's upland regions take great pride in their work, seeing it

Grindsbrook Meadows after restoration work (reproduced with permission from Mike Rhodes, Peak District National Park).

as a challenge to find the right stone for any given situation.

Most of the work today has been made possible via Lottery funding and organizations such as 'Moors for the Future', based in Castleton, Derbyshire. Moors for the Future has kindly allowed me to reproduce the following description:

It [stone-pitching] has been successfully applied on a number of sites on the Pennine Way in the Dark Peak on slopes of between 15 and 30 degrees, where the vegetation and much of the soil had been lost to trampling and resultant water action, leaving a path of loose gravel and boulders. A good stone-pitched path will provide a stable and comfortable surface for walkers whilst reducing the visual scar considerably. The technique of stone pitching involves positioning large, locally derived blocks of undressed stone on the path line to create a series of irregular steps up the eroded slope. Where suitable stone is not available in situ, nearby screes, old quarry spoil or even abandoned dry-stone walls may provide a source.

The stones are dug into the subsoil with a flat face uppermost, wedged together to give mutual strength, and any gaps are back-filled and then covered with soil. Drainage channels are incorporated into the construction design, and the finished path surface should rise smoothly without an abrupt change of gradient, blending naturally into the hillside. The sides of the erosion scar will be landscaped and turved, and the whole area seeded with a nurse crop mix.

The most important path technique for creating miles of dry, firm 'causeway' is the laying of reclaimed mill flags across areas of deep peat to form causey paths. In terms of distance covered, this has the greatest significance.

As the majority of the UK's local authorities adopt this proven, sustainable technique for their abundantly visited upland areas, the landscape is now able to rest and mature. Although I have only concentrated on a few examples here, it does not make the work in other national parks, areas of outstanding natural beauty and nature reserves any less important. For the moment the frustrations of past erosion are being met head on, which is no bad thing, because the pressure on the British countryside has long required a symbiosis with terrain and visitor.

Paths across Peat: 'Causey Paths'

Causey paths are made out of large stone slabs (or flags) of about 11sq ft (1sq m) and 4in (10cm) thick, and are mainly laid across wet peat bogs. The large surface area of each flag allows it to be laid directly on to deep peat without its sinking. Materials usually consist of reclaimed flooring from old buildings, delivered to the nearest access point by lorry and then airlifted to the site by helicopter. The stone is extremely heavy, demanding a team of five workers to construct the path, with at least three of them laying one flag; the actual laying of the stone is simple, but manoeuvring one around the work area can be tricky.

The following notes give technical details of the methods used by the Pennine Way Management Project (PWMP) in the Peak District National Park. The information it contains is relevant to most upland path projects, which is why I have included it here: *Technical Guidelines*, by Mike Rhodes, Peak District National Park Authority and reproduced by his kind permission.

1. Path Repair Techniques

The Pennine Way in the Peak District crosses a variety of different terrain types, and the impacts that the trail has on the landscape, and the techniques used to minimize those impacts, reflect this. There are broadly three types of terrain where the impacts are severe, and their main characteristics can be summarized as follows:

Shallow gradient blanket peat: Poorly drained and wet for much of the year, these peat soils are therefore vulnerable to trampling damage to great widths, with consequent loss of soil structure and vegetation. Walking becomes unpleasant, and where the route is especially popular, damage has significantly affected the fragile ecology by vegetation loss and wildlife disturbance.

About half of the Pennine Way in the Peak District (20 miles/32km) crosses terrain of this type; for example, on:

- Kinder Scout Plateau
- Mill Hill to the Snake Pass
- Alport Low
- Dun Hill and Black Hill
- Marsden Moor and Saddleworth Moor

Steep gradient (10 degrees) mineral soil/shallow peat: Although limited in extent, steep slopes form important features of the route, and the sections of route crossing them have suffered exten-

sive soil loss as a result of the friability of the soil. Rock and turf displacement may be hazardous to the unwary walker, and visual scarring is often severe with rainwater gullies and landslides, and apparent from great distances.

Such sections of route include those at:

- Ashop Head
- Torside Clough Edge (Reaps Farm)
- Laddow Rocks
- Black Hill north-east shoulder
- Wessenden Head Moor (Dean Clough)

Shallow gradient mineral soil: These soils are freer draining than the peat and are therefore generally more resistant to compaction and the vegetation more able to resist trampling. However, they have still suffered extensive loss by gullying, and visual intrusion is high, due to the particular popularity of the sites, and the nature and range of use.

About one third of the route (15 miles/24km) crosses such terrain, for example at:
- Grindsbrook Clough
- Broadlee Bank
- Kinder Scout edges
- Devil's Dike
- Wildboar Grain
- Black Hill plateau edges

Techniques

There has been a range of techniques developed to deal with the differing terrain types and use levels. These are:

Stone-Flag Surfacing
The Pennine Way Management Project (PWMP) has revived the traditional method of laying stone flags in order to repair eroded footpaths on shallow-

gradient blanket peat. This technique, developed centuries ago, has many advantages for the modern path builder, and has proved durable and popular.

The method of laying stone-flag paths, known locally as 'causey' paths, evolved during the Middle Ages and continued until the industrial revolution as a means of improving transport links for the pack-horse trains across the boggy moors. These old causeys were built using the local sandstone and gritstone, which is easily dressed to large flat flags about 2ft (60cm) wide. Streams were crossed with large flags to form clapper bridges. The best known examples of these medieval causeys in the Dark Peak are on the Long Causeway, Doctor's Gate and below Derwent Edge.

Small-scale trials to recreate existing causey paths in Calderdale were carried out on the Pennine Way near Hebden Bridge in the late 1980s. Although successful, it was not until a large supply of suitable stone was found that the technique was adopted by the PWMP, as the best way of dealing with the problems of creating a durable path across deep peat.

The advantages of flagstones over other deep peat surfacing techniques are, first, the stone is native to the southern Pennine: some paths have been built using aggregates such as limestone or basalt, which not only look intrusive in a moorland setting, but can also affect adjacent vegetation by the leaching of minerals. Second, the flags are recycled from demolition sites; they are therefore

flags are laid side by side to form a durable walkway. the joins are packed with soil – can be reseeded.

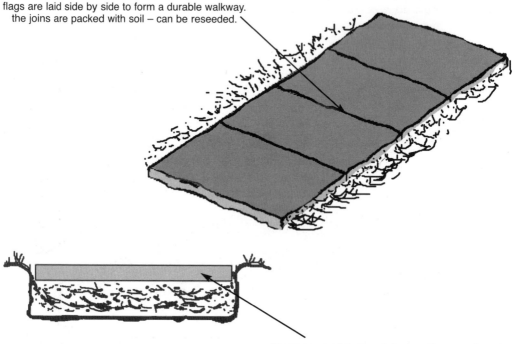

flagstones set into foundation, resting on soft peat.

Laying flags for 'causey-paths'.

relatively cheap, and do not have the impact on the local environment of newly quarried stone. The recycled stone has the benefits of 150 years of ageing, which gives it a weathered look and provides a hardened patina, making it more durable. The unevenness of the hewn or naturally rippled surface provides good grip even in wet weather.

The flags can be laid directly on the eroded peat surface without the need for an underlay or geotextile, because the size of each stone spreads the surface-area loading. This minimizes cost and eliminates the need to bring man-made materials on to the moor.

Unlike unconsolidated aggregate, the solid stone flag does not suffer from sur-face wash-out by rainwater. This quality minimizes the requirement for drainage works, such as ditching, which alter the natural water flow and can lower the water table of a mire. It also reduces the requirement for maintenance.

Small watercourses across the path can be crossed using longer flags as 'clapper bridges', without the necessity of pipes or other intrusive engineering structures.

The estimated lifespan of a maintained flag path is five times that of aggregate and ten times that of wooden boardwalk.

Laying the flagstones requires a combination of physical strength and an understanding of the aesthetics of both the stone and the moorland setting. The

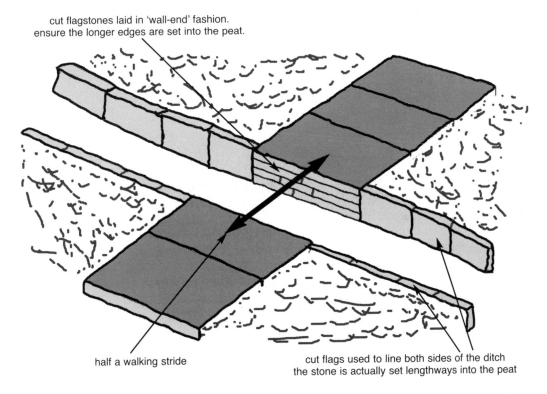

cut flagstones laid in 'wall-end' fashion.
ensure the longer edges are set into the peat.

half a walking stride

cut flags used to line both sides of the ditch
the stone is actually set lengthways into the peat

Simple 'step-over' drainage method.

reclaimed stone comes ready dressed into different sizes, with an average thickness of 4in (100mm) and width of 3ft 3in (1m). Length can be from 20in to 5ft (0.5m to 1.5m). The dimensions are important – if they are too small, the stones don't bed properly on to the soil surface and may rock or sink; however, the larger stones (at up to 0.5 tons each) are difficult to get into position. The flags are butted together to provide mutual support, and limit the potential for creating trip points.

On fibrous peat, or where they can be laid on intact vegetation, the flags are laid directly on to the surface, with some levelling and ground preparation using spades or mattocks. On very wet, amorphous peat the flags are generally laid proud of the surface to allow settling, but on mineral soils they are dug in flush with the ground surface.

Experienced staff understand that the aesthetics of a flag path are important, not only to its appearance but also to the comfort of the user. The stones should be level with each other with an even edge. The path line should conform to the undulations and curves of the existing path-line, to follow the preferred walk-line, prevent unnaturally straight lines, and break up the visual impact. Turf from nearby is generally brought to the path sides to improve both the visual appearance of the new path and to promote revegetation of the eroded line.

Flag paths have been most successful at repairing paths crossing the blanket mires at gradients of less than 5 degrees. However, flagstones have also been successfully employed on eroded mineral soils and on gradients of up to 10 degrees. Occasional problems have been encountered by ice, where surface water has crossed the path; but generally the paths remain dry and comfortable to use all year.

Maintenance is minimal – the occasional resetting of a tilted flag is all that is required.

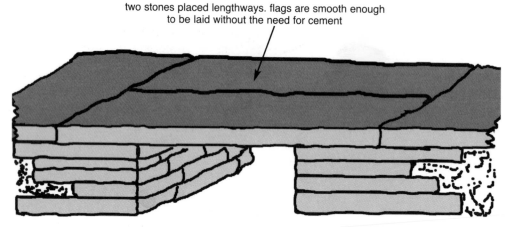

two stones placed lengthways. flags are smooth enough to be laid without the need for cement

bridge supports (called abutments) constructed like dry stone wall-ends ensure that the stone is laid with their longer edges into the peat

Small flagstone bridge.

Machine Repairs to Mineral Soil Paths

Where a damaged stretch of path cuts through free-draining mineral subsoil on a gradient of less than 15 degrees, it is possible to reduce the erosion scar and provide a reasonably sustainable path by carrying out landscaping and drainage work with a mini-digger.

The aim of this repair work is to prevent further soil loss from trampling and water erosion, and to provide a sustainable walking surface using the existing exposed mineral subsoil as the path surface. The erosion scar is reduced to a path width of about 5ft (1.5m) by revegetation and stabilization of the sides of the path.

These goals are achieved in a number of ways by:

- Reprofiling and levelling the eroded path surface.
- Providing adequate drainage of the path by top/cross-ditching and culverts.
- Cambering to ensure any surface water is taken off the path and not allowed to run along the surface.
- Blocking off multiple walk-lines with turf and boulders.
- Seeding the new path's sides and ditch.

This technique has the advantages of being extremely cheap, there being little importation of surfacing material (some stone may be required for culverts), and labour costs are minimal. The minimum use of materials ensures that with care, the finished path will have a sympathetic, natural look. It does, however, depend on careful analysis of the sub-soil to ensure that the resultant path surface will be adequately free draining and durable.

Hand Working Using insitu Materials

On some sites it is possible to reduce the impacts of recreation, to reduce the width of damage or the number of braided lines, and prevent any further deterioration, by the simple manipulation of surface materials. Experienced and skilled path workers are able to achieve substantial reductions in path width and disturbance by this technique. This may be desirable in particularly remote or sensitive sites to avoid any visual intrusion by imported surfacing, or to avoid the appearance of making the path 'easier' to negotiate. A number of methods of work have been employed to solve these problems, and these can be loosely bracketed together under the heading 'hand-work'; these will include:

Drainage: The control of the action of water is fundamental to path management, as boggy paths deteriorate more rapidly, cause people to spread out laterally, and surfaces to scour.

Realignment: Some subtle realigning of the path on to more durable ground by the positioning of boulders or turf banks to block off damaged routes. Surfacing of short stretches may be necessary to firm the path surface and keep people on the desired route – this can be achieved by gathering nearby stone and gravel to produce a natural-looking path.

Revegetation: Controls on sheep grazing have helped to reduce vegetation damage, but the localized addition of seed and fertilizer and transplanted vegetation will help further to maintain a healthy sward and begin the process of revegetation. To achieve the required aesthetic level and attention to detail, the work is necessarily labour-intensive, but costs are minimized by there being a requirement to import few materials. The result will be a path that is reduced in width and impact, yet capable of sustaining the current levels of use whilst retaining a natural appearance in keeping with the high quality landscape.

Aggregates

Aggregates have only rarely been used by the PWMP, for reasons outlined above. However, grit-stone aggregate has been used where either the soil is too clay or organic to use as a path surface, or the slope is too steep for flagstones, but not steep enough for pitching. In the latter cases unsorted grit-stone aggregates have been mixed with the subsoil and compacted, to create a consolidated surface. This technique is quite different from the use of sorted aggregates of non-native geology, laid on geotextile: this was the favoured technique prior to 1991, but is now considered to be unsuitable.

Long-Term Maintenance

Where a path has been constructed and, in particular, where vegetation reinstatement work has been carried out, a regular programme of maintenance is necessary to ensure that the initial capital investment is protected and the work is effective over the longer term. Regular checks are essential on newly constructed sections of path, particularly during the first year or two after construction and reinstatement whilst the new path settles. These inspections will look at:

Drainage: It is important to ensure that the drainage system is functioning properly, that water breaks and culverts are clear, and that water is kept off the path.

Path surface: Checks will indicate whether the surface is proving adequate and people are keeping to it. If not, more landscaping may be required.

Revegetation: Some seeded areas may require a top dressing of seed or fertilizer to provide full cover.

Since 1997, the PWMP has carried out a full programme of path maintenance, based on regular inspections of the route. This work is funded at 75 per cent by the Countryside Agency, and 25 per cent by the National Park Ranger Service, and is expected to continue for the foreseeable future.

2. Revegetation

Many parts of the Pennine Way in the Peak District had suffered such extensive areas of trampling that, without assistance, natural recovery of the vegetation would have been minimal or non-existent. Therefore, in order to achieve the overall aims of the project, revegetation work had to be carried out in conjunction with the surfacing of the footpath.

Revegetation of damaged moorland in the Peak District has been the study of the Moorland Management Project (MMP), and others, since 1983. The Pennine Way Management Project has developed recommendations from their reports in order to revegetate large areas of moorland damaged by trampling. The main published sources were MMP Phase 2 (Tallis and Yalden, 1983) and Phase 3 reports (Anderson, *et al.*, 1997); and The National Trust High Peak Estate (National Trust, 1993 and Trotter, 1997).

The Difficulties of Restoration

Revegetation of bare, trampled ground on the Pennine Way presents particular difficulties, for the following reasons:

Instability: Bare peat is subject to severe wind, rain and frost erosion, even on shallow gradients, and must be stabilized to allow revegetation.

Acidity: The moorland plateau of the Peak District has total inputs of atmospheric pollution (mainly sulphur and nitrogen) probably as high as anywhere in the UK (Anderson *et al.*, 1997). This is due to a combination of the prevailing winds coming from industrial Manchester, and acid concentration in mist and high rainfall. The pH of southern Pennine peat is typically between 2.8 and 3.4, whereas a minimum of 3.5 to 3.7 is required to establish desired species.

Lack of seedbank: Large areas of bare peat rarely have residual seed, especially when heavily trampled, and may be distant from native seed sources. Seed and transplanted material will usually have to be imported.

Grazing: Grazing pressure can have a considerable effect on the quality of moorland vegetation, as to whether it flowers and fruits well, and whether it is vigorous and spreading. Sheep grazing tends to be high around bare peat areas even in a generally low background grazing pressure, as sheep tend to gather around the mineral edges, weakening and breaking the sward. Therefore for revegetation to be successful, any remnant vegetation should be protected and encouraged.

Trampling: Fragile seedlings and transplants are particularly prone to damage by trampling, whether by humans or animals. The path must therefore be re-routed or re-surfaced and sheep excluded from the damaged area prior to restoration.

Logistics: The remoteness of the sites and the requirement of a high level of inputs mean that labour and transport costs are high and logistics difficult. Large remote sites are harder to restore because the work cannot be effectively achieved by hand, and they may not be accessible to machines to spread the seed, lime and fertilizer mechanically.

Technical Approaches

The approaches to restoration will therefore be dependent upon an assessment of individual site conditions. Ranges of treatments are available which may be implemented successively, depending on the complexity of the specific restoration problem. These are:

The Exclusion of Stock

Stock grazing is almost always a problem on the Dark Peak moorlands, and even when sheep numbers are low there will be preferential grazing of establishing plants. Only rarely has revegetation been achieved without stock control, but even this has been much slower than if fencing had been erected. The most economical way of revegetating damaged moorland is to exploit any surviving vegetation as a source for establishing new plants. Hence it is important to protect whatever survives against any further damage from grazing, trampling and mechanical damage. On partially bare mineral soils in the

Dark Peak, even with steep slopes and little stability at higher altitudes, vegetation returns relatively quickly once protected from grazing. Bare peat is very difficult to revegetate where it is deep, mobile and exposed, particularly at high altitude; here, fencing to exclude sheep seems to be essential.

Where enclosure is impractical, it may be possible to distract sheep away from damaged areas by better management elsewhere (e.g. many smaller burns in the heather) or by shepherding. Alternatively, sheep should be removed completely from the moor from October to April, which is when most damage to young heather takes place.

Artificial Seeding with Heather and/or Grasses

Large bare areas may lack a seed source, in which case heather seed is probably the most appropriate species to use for revegetation if a dwarf-shrub heath is the objective. Heather forms a crucial component of the moorland landscape and is, furthermore, the only native dwarf-shrub species in this region that produces large quantities of collectable seed. Although not yet commercially available on a large scale, heather seed is collected locally. Wavy hair-grass can be a major seed source from remnant moorland vegetation, but for seed to be collected in large quantities requires considerable inputs of labour. There appear to be no other native moorland species that are both a profuse source of seed and suitable for use in moorland restoration.

In the more difficult situations (e.g. deep peat), use of a nurse crop of commercial grass seed is necessary (together with lime and fertilizer) to limit erosion while heather is establishing itself.

English Nature has produced guidelines on the use of supplementary seed sources in moorland revegetation schemes in especially sensitive areas such as SSSIs (English Nature, 1995). These guidelines are summarized thus:

- Natural colonization from local seed sources is the preferred method of revegetation of bare ground, where there is no immediate necessity for stabilization and where there is evidence of an adequate seed bank. Where it is considered necessary to introduce seed to stabilize bare ground, locally derived seed is again the preferred method.
- If locally derived seed is not available, preference should be given to seed mixes containing a predominance of alien (i.e. non-moorland) species, to prevent the possibility of hybridization, establishment and spread – for example, perennial rye grass (*Lolium perenne*) and meadow grasses *Poa* spp. Seed mixes containing bent and fescue grasses (*Agrostis* and *Festuca* spp.) should be avoided if possible, as there is much concern about the propensity for bent/fescue cultivars (i.e. non-native strains) to hybridize with the local flora. Even supposedly native seed is often of non-British (European or North American) provenance.
- Where prevention of erosion is the prime concern, the aim should be to utilize nurse grasses with a life expectancy of only two to five years in the upland environment. These will be predominantly ryegrasses and meadow grasses.

Transplanting

Transplants of adjacent moorland vegetation have been tried, with varying degrees of success, in a number of trials in the Peak District. The success of transplanting plants of crowberry, bilberry, cross-leaved heath, common cotton-grass and heather depends on a number of factors, such as soil moisture and mineral composition, grazing and turf size. Practicality also plays a large consideration, as transplanting is very labour intensive. It does, however, provide an important role in establishing native vegetation into a nurse crop or a very large bare area where the available native seed source is limited. The use of turf has to take other environmental constraints into consideration, particularly in the sourcing of material.

Application of Fertilizer and Lime

The use of nurse grasses and of certain moorland transplants (for example, common cotton-grass) requires the addition of lime and fertilizer.

Various NPK fertilizers have been used in Dark Peak revegetation programmes, at applications varying from 440 to 1,100lb (200 to 500kg) per hectare. Preference is for slow-release high-phosphorus fertilizers (e.g. Enmag), or for supplementary phosphorus fertilizers.

Lime applications employed in various projects have varied from 2,200 to 4,400lb (1,000 to 2,000kg) per hectare. Higher dosage is desirable at least for deep peat areas, to counteract the very high acidity; prior determinations of soil pH and nutrient levels will help to decide whether additional lime and fertilizer is necessary or not.

Again, certain general recommendations have been made by English Nature that should be followed wherever possible:

1. Lime is applied to increase ion exchange in the soil/peat, and hence to increase nutrient uptake by the plants. It is not intended to increase the soil pH, except in extreme conditions (e.g. eroding blanket peat), and hence in general it should be applied as a one-off treatment.
2. Slow-release fertilizers with low nitrogen, high phosphate and medium potash content (e.g. 'Enmag' or 'Plantings Plus') are preferred.
3. Extreme caution should be exercised to prevent watercourses and areas of low-tolerance vegetation (e.g. some moss-rich areas) receiving chemical applications.

Soil Stabilization

Soil mobility is a major inhibitor of revegetation, where young seedlings are unable to root deep enough. The use of geojute and geocoir (biodegradable netting) have been used successfully to stabilize bare deep peat. Geojute netting survived for four years before disintegrating, by which time a vegetation cover of about 50 per cent had become established. Geocoir is longer lasting, but the breakdown process tends to leave unsightly strands on the moor. Heather brashings were effective in securing cut heather at a small-plot scale, but have had mixed results at a larger scale. A patch of wool mulch impregnated with grass seed was applied to deep peat in one trial, but failed to remain in place in severe winds. The geojute mesh, therefore, has proved to be the most useful material to stabilize the peat, but it is expensive, and it is also visually intrusive on a large scale and would need to be adequately stock-fenced until it decayed.

CHAPTER 12

LOWLAND PATHS AND BRIDLEWAYS

This chapter deals with lowland paths and bridleways made with aggregates and stone pitching. Although stone pitching offers a durable solution in areas with a high water table, aggregate walkways still remain the most common feature in lowland districts. They are relatively cheap to install when compared to laying vast tracts of stone slabs, and require only a basic knowledge to build. For bridleway sub-bases and surfaces, aggregates offer the best economical solution to concrete/tarmac, and the safest alternative to stone-pitched designs. Equines may cause damage to stone or injure themselves on loose rock; a common injury is broken limbs. Users of invalid carriages and wheelchairs could find it difficult to propel themselves over a pitched surface, making the aggregate option very viable for easy-to-get-to, or roadside tourist sites.

This chapter's project discusses the construction of a route suitable for all countryside users, including agricultural and horse-drawn vehicular access. You can also use these techniques to create an extremely hardwearing footpath. During the course of the text I will describe variations that could be implemented as part of a pedestrian-only trail.

There are numerous factors to consider before taking on these projects, such as the quality of the soil structure and its free-draining capabilities. Others include water run-off on slopes, and the damaging effect it can have on new surfaces. Heavy rainfall will produce streams of water that will quickly rut and destroy top surfaces. The destruction can be severe on descending sections, and techniques for minimizing these problems are discussed later. A public path will often ford small brooks or streams, and when the water table rises flooding might occur, which will wash away aggregates. These watercourses may be dry in summer and only appear in winter, usually draining from mountain summits during heavy rainfall and snow thaw, but the resulting flows play an essential role in an area's biodiversity, and any diversion could produce drastic changes to the local ecosystem. Instead, it is advisable to channel the water underneath the path by installing 'culverts' – again, this will be discussed a little later. Where a right of way crosses a river or large stream, various bridge designs can be brought into the scenario; the next chapter describes some of these solutions in detail.

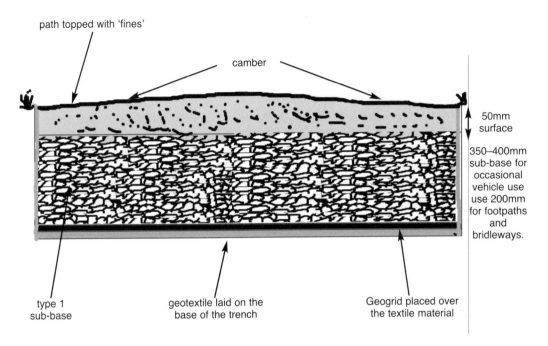

path topped with 'fines'

camber

50mm
surface

350–400mm
sub-base for
occasional
vehicle use
use 200mm
for footpaths
and
bridleways.

type 1
sub-base

geotextile laid on the
base of the trench

Geogrid placed over
the textile material

Path cross section.

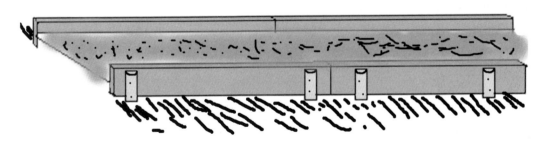

Use revetment boarding to retain the path surface.

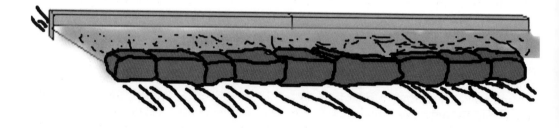

stone must be laid in a foundation trench

Stone can also be used to retain the path surface.

Before path construction goes ahead it is essential to survey the proposed site, taking note of the route's various high and low points. Most of the preparation work will involve excavating a substantial foundation for sub-surface materials, but there may be sections that require building up as opposed to digging. For these you will have to assemble some sort of aggregate containment similar to the revetments described in Chapter 4. Maybe all that is required is a single layer of one or two boards, or a few courses of dry-stone walling. On footpaths, a steeper passage may demand a few steps (described earlier) though on bridleways or tracks intended for occasional vehicle use, steps cannot be constructed, for obvious reasons.

Materials

Regardless of the future load a path is going sustain in its life, all paths require a sub-base, and strong paths are laid with two layers: a sub-base and a top surface. Bridleway users will benefit from this high specification layout, as it will afford the most hardwearing surface that basic path construction can offer. In many cases, if constructed over free-draining or drier soil structures, they are suitable for occasional motor-vehicle usage. However, it has to be said that if the intention is to build a route solely for frequent motorized access, a far stronger feature ought to be established, incorporating a substantial foundation, copious aggregates and tarmac surface – and vehicle highways are beyond this book's remit. Nevertheless, the path I am about to describe will be perfectly viable for horse-drawn vehicles, equines, wheelchairs, invalid carriages, pushchairs, pedal cycles, pedestrians, and infrequent motor-vehicle use.

The kind of aggregate used will depend on the nature of the surrounding soil. Limestone or chalk aggregates should not be considered in acid regions, as it will raise the local pH level, disturbing natural flora. Here you should import locally derived hardcore of a sandstone or clay-based content. Because our project path is going to be designed for infrequent agricultural vehicular use, the hardcore sub-base will be comprised of a 14–16in (350–400mm) layer of 'Type 1' crushed stone. This will then be compacted down using a pedestrian roller or vibrating plate. Type 1 material contains stone ranging from 3in (75mm) down to dust or 'fines'. It is the fines that help to harden the sub-base. On footpaths or bridleways you normally only need to lay a 6–8in (150–200mm) base. For invalid carriages and wheelchairs the route's surface must be smooth, therefore the path will be topped with a 2in (50mm) layer of crushed stone from $^1/_4$in (6mm) down to dust (or fines), then compacted.

For routes constructed over soft/wet ground it is recommended that you lay a path base with a 'geotextile' membrane before hardcore is brought in. There are numerous geotextile products available, and a list of websites, for your research, can be found in the 'Useful Organizations' chapter at the end of this book. Aggregate paths will decay quickly on spongy-wet soil, and basically, a geotextile membrane counters this by creating a floating sub-surface. I advise anyone who is embarking on a practical skills career to research this subject, as it is an important constructional element of path design. For the sake of continuity, I will briefly

Example of a path with a limestone surface.

Example of a path using acid-friendly aggregates. The surface is clay-based 'Hoggin', which eventually hardens to form a firm walkway.

discuss the various merits of certain geogrids and textiles in the context of the project path.

Geotextile is classified into two main types. The first includes Lotrak and Terram, made of a very fine-meshed, almost cloth-like permeable material similar to the membranes used for garden weed mulching. If laid correctly it allows moisture to rise and leach away, thereby preventing any movement of path materials. There have been successful trials on shallow peat and mineral soils, but laid over deep, waterlogged peat it could flex, causing the path eventually to sink into the softer areas. The second type is stronger and more rigid, and includes 'Geogrid' and 'Wyretex'. The larger mesh styles trap the base aggregates in the wider mesh gaps, resulting in an inflexible path foundation, ideal for softer substrata. Trials over deep peat have been successful, although fine particles can leach through the larger grid sizes.

I have already mentioned the trials that took place on the Snake Summit during the late 1980s. One of the successful exercises involved covering the foundation's base with Terram, using it as a 'separator' to trap fine stone

Hoggin blends into a sandstone region.

particles; over the top of that we laid the stronger Geogrid. We achieved a permeable base, stubborn enough to withstand the wear and tear inflicted on one of Britain's more popular walking routes, and with the durability to remain in place on one of Derbyshire's softer moorlands. Some of these trials led to the preferred stone-pitching method explained earlier. Note that on the photograph the geotex is topped with a layer of Type 1, limestone sub-base. Nowadays it is not good practice to introduce minerals of a high pH level into a naturally acidic environment.

Further materials you may need are 10ft × 6in × 2in boards and pointed stakes for revetments, not forgetting the 5in or 6in nail fixings.

The materials I have just described are more than adequate for paths that require a durable structure for equines, and for pedestrian and light motor vehicle use.

Tool Requirements

• A mechanized excavator for digging long sections of path foundation; on smaller projects, spades will do an able job.

- A wheelbarrow, mechanized barrow, or an all-terrain vehicle (ATV) capable of transporting aggregates; in drier locations a dumper truck might suffice.
- Mechanized, pedestrian roller or vibrating plate for compacting aggregates; ear protection and gloves are to be worn when operating these machines.
- Large grading rake for levelling surfaces before compaction.
- String-lines and stakes for marking path edges.
- Shovel.
- Sledgehammer.
- Tape measure.
- Long scissors or sharp knife for trimming the fabric membrane.
- Strong cutters or snips (we used tin snips) for cutting the Geogrid.

For extra features such as revetments or retaining walls, you will need the following:

- Walling hammer.
- Claw hammer.
- Spirit level and line level.
- Crowbar.
- Fencing maul.
- Hand drill or rechargeable drill for pilot holes.

Method of Construction

No path construction begins without first marking the area to be excavated. This project is going to be 4ft (1.2m) wide; footpaths can be as little 3ft (1.2m). The depth of the base will be a minimum of 15in (38cm), but 6–8in (15–20cm) will suffice on pedestrian walkways and bridleways (don't forget we are building this track to sustain occasional motor vehicle use).

Begin by staking a line on each side of the proposed route. Only mark an area that can be completed in a day's work, because open trenches left overnight or longer will soon become boggy in wet weather. Having marked the line with stakes, attach two parallel strings, one for each edge, and then tension them by tying them on to the end stakes. Work can begin by digging inside the string-lines, until the day's foundation has been excavated.

The next phase is to lay the first fabric membrane. This will come wrapped on a roll, and all you need do is lift it to the start of the trench, ensuring an equal overlap on both sides. Roll the material down the line, leaving around 6in (15cm) overlapping the front of the foundation. In windy conditions you will have to use stones or some other heavy objects to weight it down; do this every 4ft (1.2m) or so. If the weather is calm the membrane can be taken to the full extent of the dig. Do not cut the membrane; leave it on the roll for the next day's work.

The trench is now ready for the Geogrid. Geogrid sits on the bottom without any overlap, and can be quite tricky to lay due to its tendency to roll back when spread out. Again, it will require some form of weight support. Roll the grid out in stretches of around 6ft (1.8m), then import a 14in (350mm) layer of Type 1 sub-base (on footpaths this need only be 8in (200mm)). Extend the roll for a further 6ft (1.8m) and pile in more sub-base, bringing it up to the same level. As each load is dumped, it should be raked level. Try not to cover the whole section, but leave a small stretch of geotextile open to the air, ready for the next day's work.

Doing this is essential when the Geogrid has been rolled to its full extent: if it is completely covered you will not be able to overlap and tie on new grid.

Now that the sub-base has been laid and raked level, use the roller or vibrating plate to firm it down. Following the edge of the trench, start from one end, guiding the machine to the opposite end. Turn around, then make your way back to the beginning, working a fresh line next to the one just compacted. Continue in this fashion, gradually moving towards the opposing edge, until the entire section has been tamped. That was one 'pass': at least five passes are necessary to ensure sufficient compaction.

Loading the surface aggregate is very much the same as the sub-base, only on this occasion it will have to be sculpted to form a camber to aid water run-off. This isn't too difficult, and just involves dumping the material in the middle of the path and raking it towards each edge, ensuring that the centreline always remains the highest point. The surface will require at least three compaction passes.

The foregoing is a basic guide to laying a countryside path; however, the methods will have to change when obstacles such as rivers and streams and slopes are encountered (slopes and revetments have already been discussed in Chapter 4.).

Terram and Geogrid laid in a footpath foundation. The white stone on top is Type 1 sub-base.

Volunteers and staff of the Peak District National Authority excavating a footpath foundation.

A newly surfaced footpath topped with limestone dust and fines. Note the vibration plate in the background; this will be used to compact the material.

Drainage Techniques

The following sequence of drawings and illustrations sets out the basics of some simple drainage techniques.

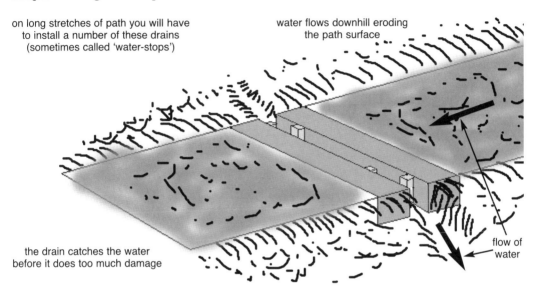

on long stretches of path you will have to install a number of these drains (sometimes called 'water-stops')

water flows downhill eroding the path surface

the drain catches the water before it does too much damage

flow of water

Simple drainage technique using railway sleepers on gradients.

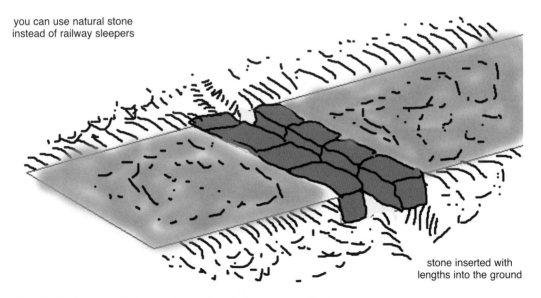

you can use natural stone instead of railway sleepers

stone inserted with lengths into the ground

Simple drainage technique using natural stone on gradients.

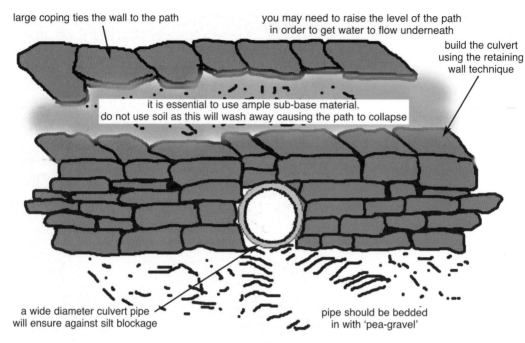

large coping ties the wall to the path

you may need to raise the level of the path in order to get water to flow underneath

build the culvert using the retaining wall technique

it is essential to use ample sub-base material.
do not use soil as this will wash away causing the path to collapse

a wide diameter culvert pipe will ensure against silt blockage

pipe should be bedded in with 'pea-gravel'

An example of a culvert.

Denbighshire Countryside Service volunteer group dealing with a drainage problem in an environmentally sensitive area. The route is a section of the Offa's Dyke long-distance footpath.

Clearing silt and adding depth to a stream can help combat flooding.

This stream used to ford the path. A culvert has been added, and the path surface has been raised slightly. Note the wide diameter of the culvert pipe. Railway sleepers instead of stone retain the path surface.

The fact that this area is an environmentally sensitive site meant that the water, which helps to feed the marsh in the background, could not be directed away from its normal course. Building culverts helps to maintain natural flow, and this sort of treatment is essential for the protection of biodiversity.

An example of a natural drain (or gully) constructed with a couple of courses of stone, work carried out by the Snowdonia National Park Authority.

Larger stone has been used to form this gully, work carried out by the Snowdonia National Park Authority.

A large stone flag spans a stream that is too wide for one comfortable walking stride, work carried out by the Snowdonia National Park Authority.

Built by a Snowdonia National Park work team, this is a superb example of a culvert, complete with dry-stone retaining walls. Note also how the stone in the background is retaining the path surface.

A Snowdonia National Park team maintaining a gully on the Miners' Track near Mount Snowdon.

The Stone-Pitched Method

An alternative to aggregate paths is the more durable stone-pitched method. These next examples are part of the work that is being carried out by the Snow-donia National Park Authority, repairing the damage caused by years of visitor pressure. Unlike the causey paths laid directly on peat, these have been placed on the top of mineral soil.

Erosion scar caused by walkers.

Using skills akin to dry-stone walling, craftsmen have laid these stones directly on to the soil below. A level foundation is initially excavated and then the stone is tightly locked together with smaller material.

You can also use aggregates to fill in the gaps.

A finished section of path that will last for decades.

CHAPTER 13

FOOTBRIDGES

This chapter concentrates solely on foot-bridges subjected to only light use. Vehicle structures, and furniture intended for a high-volume visitor load (bridges expected to support many people at the same time) and equines, must be designed by a civil engineer and installed by experienced staff or contractors. By the term 'light use' I am describing a feature under 30ft (9m) in length, suitable for only low use. Most footbridges on public rights of way fall into this latter group and can be erected by experienced work teams, volunteers or countryside contractors. The structures I will describe later are only suitable for shallow crossings where it is easy to work in the water wearing wellingtons. I have chosen to describe these for two reasons: firstly, this type of crossing is most common; secondly, a full text description of every single style of bridge would be a publication in its own right.

The site for a bridge has to be chosen carefully, and it involves an accurate survey of the proposed crossing. Various public bodies may have to be consulted too, including the HSE, who have the right to inspect the bridge at any time. Permission should be sought from the Highways Authority if the footbridge is going to become part of the rights-of-way network, and from the Environment Agency (in Scotland consult with the River Purification Board). The Environment Agency will advise on local flooding levels, as this will dictate how high the crossing must be in relation to changing water levels. In Scotland, planning permission may need to be granted before work commences.

Choosing the Right Site

The philosophy of adhering to a path's definitive line may in some cases be difficult, resulting in the possibility of having to apply for a 'Footpath Diversion Order'. Footbridges have to be sited away from bends where there is a danger of erosion, and the riverbanks should be solid enough to support the abutments.

Having found the ideal site, two people will have to survey the crossing to attain accurate levels for the bridge abutments. On shallow brooks and streams you can use two steel poles (called 'ranging poles') of around 4ft (1.2m) in length, hammered into the ground on either of the stream. You also need a string-line and line level. Set the poles back about 2ft (60cm) from the point where the riverbanks begin to level out with land, and ensure they are vertical by testing them with a spirit level.

Next, tie the string to one pole, preferably the one on the highest bank. Make sure the string is at ground level. Pull the string to the opposite pole. With the line held taught, a second person could attach the line level, giving instructions to raise or lower the string. When levels have been achieved, mark the exact point on the ranging pole. Measure the distance from ground level to the mark and note it down, and then drive in a stake, sawing it down to that level. The top of the stake represents the base on which the bridge will rest on this side of the stream.

Choosing the Bridge

Footbridge Terms

Abutment: Support at each end of the bridge.
Pier: Intermediate support for the footbridge constructed between the abutments.
Deck: The walking surface of the footbridge.
Live load: The load caused by users when walking across the bridge.
Dead load: The weight of the entire footbridge when resting on the abutments.
Stringers: The beams that support the deck.
Superstructure: The upper part of the footbridge including the deck, the deck supports and handrails.
Substructure: The abutments and piers that support the bridge.

The style of the bridge will be dependent on the length and height of the crossing. Simple bridges can span very narrow brooks with shallow banks, where there is no danger to users. These are low structures that do not usually require a stone-built abutment. Furniture here includes sleeper bridges and small duckboard affairs.

Bridges with a high water-level clearance of around 4ft (1.2m) demand the use of safety railing. These are much heavier and require a stone abutment. Recommended materials can be purchased from specialist suppliers or dedicated sawmills with experience of producing products for countryside use. Ideally the timber should be treated hardwood, although some safe units are supplied in softwood. Recycled railway sleepers, without stringers, make useful decks on simple crossings, but duckboard bridges must have stringer support. Large hand-railed bridges are best purchased in kit form as they should be manufactured to the correct specifications demanded by the Highways Authority and the HSE.

Building a Simple Sleeper-style Bridge

Materials

- 2 × recycled railway sleepers or 2 × custom-manufactured deck planks if the span is wider. Both styles are very heavy objects, requiring care when lifting.
- 2 × 3ft × 4in × 4in square unpointed posts. These will act as simple abutments for the deck. Hardwood posts are recommended.
- 4 × 3ft × 4in × 4in pointed or unpointed posts. These are dug into the ground and bolted to the abutments. Treated hardwood is recommended, but treated softwood is an alternative.
- About 10ft (3m) of threaded rod.

- 16 × nuts and 16 × washers. Used to connect the structure to abutments and posts.

The bridge will also require some form of friction or anti-skid solution. Wet railway sleepers are hazardous, and all algae-covered timber can be slippery. A popular method is to affix chicken wire or fencing staples, but the best solution, in my opinion, is to exploit the benefits of purpose-made friction treads. The material, similar to roofing felt in appearance, can be cut to size and secured with 'clout nails'. It is also a good idea to coat ground-level timber with a suitable treatment.

Tool Requirements

- Spade.
- Fencing maul.
- Crowbar.
- Tamper.
- Wrench suitable for locking down the bridge's connecting nuts.
- Tape measure.
- Hacksaw for trimming the threaded rod to size.
- Woodsaw.
- Long spirit level.
- Claw hammer.
- Hand drill, brace or rechargeable drill.
- Two wood augur bits. One will be for

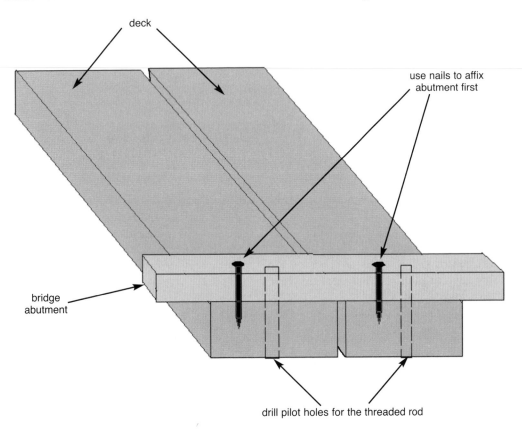

deck

use nails to affix abutment first

bridge abutment

drill pilot holes for the threaded rod

Sleeper bridge – step 1.

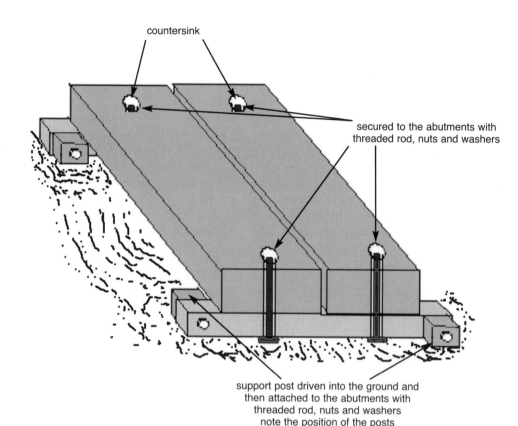

countersink

secured to the abutments with
threaded rod, nuts and washers

support post driven into the ground and
then attached to the abutments with
threaded rod, nuts and washers
note the position of the posts

Sleeper bridge – step 2.

drilling through the timbers so that threaded rod can be used; the other is for countersinking, and must be wider than the diameter of the locking nuts and washers.

- Strong rope to be used for carrying heavy materials.

Method of Construction

This project assumes a level riverbank on each side.

Bridges like this are best constructed on site, then lifted into position by at least four people. Begin by laying the two decks side by side, on even ground. Next,

adjust them until you achieve an equal 0.5in (1.2cm) gap from end to end. Take one of the timber abutments and place it so it is flush with one end of the decks. Adjust the abutment until you have an even overhang on each side.

The next job is to drill the timber for the threaded rod, but before this insert some waste wood between the ground and decks. Working with the drill and augur-bit, find the centre of the abutment in relation to the two decks, and then bore two pilot holes, one for each sleeper. Whilst drilling you should let the augur penetrate the sleepers to mark the position of holes that will need to be bored through them. After creating the pilot holes through the sleeper, repeat the process at the opposite end. You should now tack the abutments to the deck by driving in four 5in (13cm) nails, one for each sleeper end. This is a temporary fixing, bracing the bridge so it can be moved without becoming misaligned.

Up to this point the bridge has been upside down; now is the time to turn it the right way up. This manoeuvre can be dangerous and will require four people, two at each end. Nevertheless, the fact that you nailed the timber to the decks means the structure is rigid enough to cope with the adjustment. As soon as the deck faces upwards, insert the bigger augur bit into the drill and

counter-sink a depth that is relative to the height of the threaded rod's locking nuts.

The next phase will involve bolting the bridge sections together, and you will need to have access to the underside of the bridge in order to tighten the nuts. Rather than lift the structure a second time, rest each end on stable chocks. Having done that, measure from the surface of the deck to the bottom of the abutment, and then add at least 1in (2.5cm). Mark this measurement on one of the threaded rods, but do not saw it to size yet; instead, attach a nut and washer, twisting them to the level of the mark. Now insert the rod through one of the drill holes until the nut rests in the countersink.

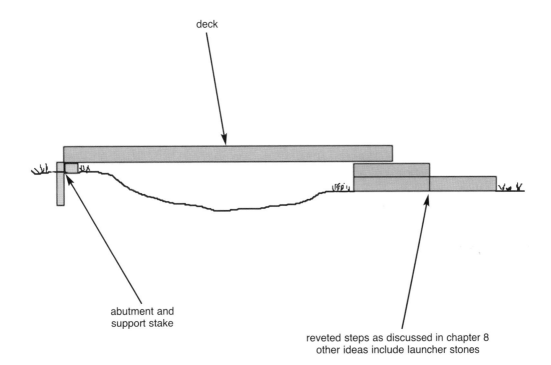

deck

abutment and
support stake

reveted steps as discussed in chapter 8
other ideas include launcher stones

Customising for irregular riverbank levels.

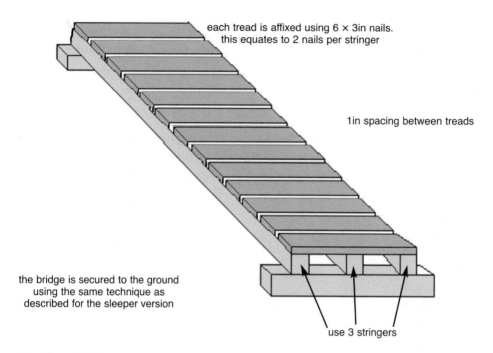

each tread is affixed using 6 × 3in nails.
this equates to 2 nails per stringer

1in spacing between treads

the bridge is secured to the ground
using the same technique as
described for the sleeper version

use 3 stringers

Duckboard bridge.

wooden abutment drilled for threaded rod on all four corners
use masonry bit to drill through the stone to a depth of at least 8in
widen the stone holes so that you can pack them with concrete
leave to set for 24 hours and then lock the bridge into position
with nuts and washers fixed to the top of the rods

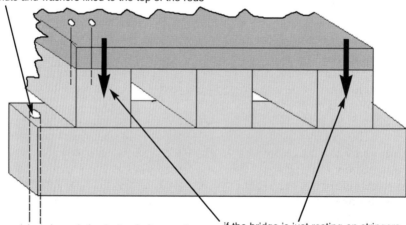

you can use a quick-drying solution instead of concrete
this is applied using a pistol grip applicator – it can be
quite toxic

if the bridge is just resting on stringers, concrete
the threaded rod to the stone via these points
larger foootbridges are connected in ths way

Securing duckboard bridge to stone abutments.

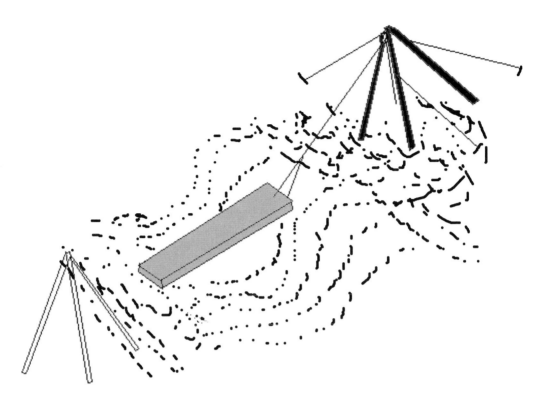

The deck for large bridges may have to be hauled to the opposite bank with winches and pulleys. Sometimes a heavy structure may have to be airlifted to the work site if access is unsuitable for 4WD vehicles and trailers.

Concentrating on the underside for a second time, ensure the rod has at least 1in clearance; you will need this in order to thread the lower nut on securely. The rod can be adjusted by turning the upper nut you have just attached. When you are sure of the correct length, remove the rod and saw it to size using a hacksaw. You can now employ the sawn section as a template for the remaining three rods. Before you insert the threaded rods, attach a washer and nut to each one. Lastly, push the ends through the holes, attach the remaining nuts and washers, and tighten them up with a wrench.

The last phase deals with moving the bridge to span the stream, and connecting the abutments to the ground stakes. This part of the task poses the greatest risk and calls for careful planning and organization. Even though the structure is lightweight (by footbridge standards), caution must be heeded when manoeuvring it to the opposite bank. Normally a bridge this size can be carried by four people; larger furniture will require some sort of lifting rig (*see* the diagrams for details).

Assuming the bridge is now spanning the stream, its levels must be inspected and the decks aligned so there is a firm soil base under both abutments. Having done that, it is time to dig in the four 3ft (90cm) support posts. These will eventually be connected to the abutment overhangs and secured with threaded rod, nuts and washers. The holes can be dug with the bridge in position, and should be excavated to a depth of at least 2ft (60cm). The location of the supports is critical: if, for example, one stake were connected to the outside left of one abutment, then the second post must be bolted to the inside right of the same abut-

ment on the other side. The technique just described will restrict future movement and possibly cut down on maintenance times. When firming in support posts, use alternate layers of tamped soil and stone.

The last jobs are drilling the posts and abutments, then locking them together with threaded rod, nuts and washers. To finish, saw the supports level with the top of the abutments, and add anti-skid material to the deck.

Heavyweight footbridges have to rest on solid abutments. Bridge abutments can be made out of concrete, but in the countryside use natural stone. Natural stone abutments should be constructed by experienced work teams. The use of handrails is a safety requirement on structures that are 4ft (1.2m) above the water level. This bridge was constructed by the Peak National Park.

Every bridge section should be connected using nuts, bolts and washers. Screws and nails do not make safe, efficient fixings. Note the fixings in the top right of the photograph: this is where the substructure is joined to the stone abutment.

Handrails should be built using 4 × 2in (10 × 5cm) treated timber rails.

The handrail (or superstructure) is supported by 4 × 4in (10 × 10cm) horizontal timbers. The diagonal timber in the picture is one of the outside struts bracing the handrail.

A clear view of the bridge's substructure and superstructure. The purpose of the central, horizontal timber underneath the deck is to support the handrail. The top rail has been smoothed and chamfered on the edges.

Another style of footbridge, resting on stone abutments. There are two points worthy of note here. Firstly, the abutment has been customized to take account of the higher riverbank. Secondly, and the most important point, the lower left of the abutment is beginning to erode, an example of 'scour' caused by flowing water. Stone toe protection would have minimized this effect.

A perfect example of a sleeper bridge resting on natural stone abutments.

Moving heavy bridge materials around the work site can be dangerous. This is a good example of how to do it correctly.

This bridge, built by volunteers in the Peak District National Park, is designed for very occasional vehicle traffic. Stringers are support by stone-filled gabions set into the riverbed.

CHAPTER 14

FINGERPOSTS AND WAY MARKS

Accurately directing walkers across private land is essential. Many access problems are a result of confusing path lines, or of tracks that are not well defined on the ground. The addition of simple way markers and fingerposts will effectively solve these issues. Most countryside and ranger services create their own fingerposts and set them in on site. Here are a couple of standard examples used throughout the UK.

Fingerposts are created out of hardwood. The size of the post is 8ft × 4in × 4in (2.4m × 10cm × 10cm). This post has been set up ready for the 'finger' to be inserted.

Fingers should be mortised into the centre of the post, somewhere near the top. The easiest method to define the mortise area is to place the end of the finger on the post, and scribe around the timber.

You should first pre-drill the mortise before cutting out the waste with a mallet and chisel.

Slotting the finger into the mortise.

Once the finger has been securely inserted, drill two holes through the post and the finger.

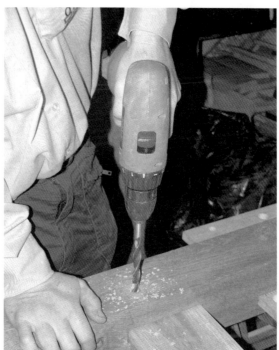

Wooden dowel of the same diameter of the drill bit is pushed and tapped through the holes.

This is a standard way marker. The angle is showing the direction of the path. Footpath way marks are coloured yellow, bridleways are blue, and restrictive path way marks are white. Long-distance paths or national trails are depicted by an acorn symbol.

USEFUL ORGANIZATIONS

The following websites provide interesting information and news on current conservation issues.

British Trust for Conservation Volunteers (BTCV)
Registered Charity (261009)
36 St Mary's Street
Wallingford
OX10 0EU
Telephone: 01491 821600
The BTCV is Britain's largest volunteer conservation body. It offers training courses on every aspect of practical conservation, and works alongside local authorities, national parks and industry (to name but a few) on practical conservation projects. This highly professional and well organized body offers a range of conservation holidays both at home and abroad. The vast range of skills, which can be practised through this organization, is boundless. To find out about the BTCV in your local area use the contact address above.

Peak District National Park Authority
Aldern House
Bakewell
Derbyshire
The Peak District National Park offers many volunteering opportunities. They run a number of conservation projects during the week and at weekends, and offer the chance to learn new skills or enhance existing ones. Brunt's Barn, their purpose-built volunteers centre, is second to none, and their highly trained full-time and part-time staff are always eager to pass on their skills and expertise.

Other Authorities

This section includes other national park authorities, areas of outstanding natural beauty (AONB), local authority-run country parks, and local colleges. All these authorities will have openings for volunteers, and many will have ranger-led event programmes, conservation projects and training courses. It is well worth contacting your nearest authority for details. Even if there are no official training days in place, they may respond positively to enquiries and arrange some events. The contact details can be found in the local telephone directory. Local colleges may run full-time and part-time rural skills training.

Snowdonia National Park Authority
National Park Offices
Penrhyndeudraeth
Gwynedd LL48 6LF

Health and Safety Executive
www.hse.gov.uk

DEFRA
www.defra.gov.uk

Campaign for the Protection of Rural England (CPRE)
www.greenchannel.com/cpre

Campaign for the Protection of Rural Wales (CPRW)
www.cprw.org.uk

Council for National Parks (CNP)
www.councilfornationalparks.
freeserve.co.uk

The Countryside Agency (CA)
www.countryside.gov.uk

Countryside Council for Wales (CCW)
www.ccw.gov.uk

The Crowood Press
www.crowood.com

Geotextiles
www.geotextile.com

ParkRanger.co.uk
www.parkranger.co.uk

Moors for the Future Partnership
The Information Centre
Buxton Road
Castleton
S33 8WP
www.moorsforthefuture.org.uk

The Institute of Public Rights of Way Officers
www.iprow.co.uk

The Ramblers Association
www.ramblers.org.uk

British Upland Footpath Trust
http://users.pandora.be/
quarsan/trails/buft.html

The National Trust
www.nationaltrust.org.uk

Countryside Jobs Link
A definitive online guide to the latest countryside jobs.
www.coumtrysidejobslink.co.uk

Ranger Jobs UK
www.rangerjobs.co.uk

GLOSSARY

stone and wooden revetments: Features designed to retain soil or path surfaces.

Timber and Stone Steps

landing: Large flat area, usually built into step-lines for comfortable ascents.
platform: The top walking surface of a step.
riser: The name given for a step, or the front of a step.

Stone Stile and Walling Terms

A-frame, batter frame: A wooden device used as a guide for building a wall to the correct angle or batter.
batter: The angle on which a wall is constructed.
bolt hole: Small access point at the base of a wall for the purpose of catching rabbits.
bridging joins: The process of crossing the joins of face-stones on a dry-stone wall or mortared brick wall.
crown: The top of a Devonshire hedge, Cornish hedge and Welsh Clawdd. Usually made of turf, which is formed into a dome.
dressed stone: Stone cut on all sides to form attractive faces.
[to] dress stone: The act of cutting natural stone to any desired shape.
end stone: Large stone used for constructing a wall end.
foundation stones, foundation, footing, footings: The base of the wall.
[to] gap: The act of repairing a damaged section of wall.

hearting, harting, infill, rubble, centre stones: Small stones used to fill the gaps in the middle of the wall.
intermediate stones, face stones: Stones used to build the section of wall between the coping and foundation.
line-level: A small spirit level that can be hung from a string-line. Used as a guide for laying accurate horizontal courses.
lunkie, hogg hole, smoot, thirl, chawl hole, cripple hole: Access points through a wall to allow the passage of livestock or the shooting of game and vermin.
pinning, pinning stone, pinners, wedges: Small stones used for jamming at the back of face-stones to counter any movement.
random walling: Undressed walling stone. Stone in its natural state. Phrase used by quarries to identify dry-stone walling product.
retaining wall: A single-skinned wall usually built to stop erosion on soil banks or river sides. Retaining walls can form attractive garden features around the sides of ponds and planting beds.
runners: Long pieces of stone.
semi-dressed stone: Stone cut on one or two sides to form an attractive face.
squeeze stile: Access point on a path usually built out of two stone lintels or two wall ends.
stone step-over stile: An access point on a footpath where walkers can cross the top of a dry-stone wall without causing damage.
stone treads: Large throughs inserted through a dry-stone wall to act as steps for a stone stile.
through-band: The middle section of wall

where the majority of stones used are throughs. The through-band ties the two faces of a wall together.

thru stones, through stones, thrus, throughs: Large stones that tie both sides of a wall together. Usually placed at 6ft (1.8m) intervals along a course.

top stones, toppers, cap stone, cappers, coping stones, copeing stones, coins: The row of stones on the top of a wall.

wall end, cheek end: A secure end of a dry-stone wall.

walling: The act of building a wall. The collective name for walling stone.

walling out: A phrase used to describe the act of placing a stone on a course, and not leaving enough room to work on the other side.

weathered face: The angled front face of a walling stone. It allows rain to wash away from a wall instead of inside it.

Wooden Stile and Fencing

bar strainer: A wire straining tool ideal for tensioning barbed wire or for straining the intermediate wires, the low tensile wires on stock-netting.

barbed wire: Pointed style of top-wire, designed to prevent large livestock from damaging fence lines.

cast-iron fencing maul or mel: The fencing maul, very similar to a sledge hammer, is specifically designed to drive fencing stakes into the ground manually.

fencing pliers: Multipurpose fencing tool incorporating a wire strainer, wire cutter, hammer, a gouge for loosing staples and a jaw for pulling them.

monkey strainer, automatic strainer: A specialist tool designed for straining wire and netting.

sheep netting, pig netting, stock netting, stock-wire: Wire netting, comprising a series of interlocking squares, used to enclose livestock.

slate fence, flagged wall: Large, flat pieces of slate inset into the ground to form a stock barrier.

straining post: Large post for attaching netting or single wire, inserted every 80ft (25m) along a proposed fence line (or where there is a change of direction or terrain height). The straining post should be set at least 3ft (1m) into the ground if possible. Fencing wire is tensioned from one strainer to the next.

top wire: A separate length of wire usually secured above netting to discourage livestock from leaning over a fence. Top wire can be plain or barbed.

Footbridges

abutment: Support at each end of the footbridge.

dead loading: The self-weight of the footbridge resting on the abutments and piers.

deck: The surface of the footbridge that users walk or ride on.

live loading: The load imposed on the footbridge by users.

piers: Intermediate supports for the footbridge superstructure between the abutments.

shuttering boards: Usually timber; they make up the boxwork into which concrete is cast.

stringers: Beams that support the deck. May be timber or steel.

substructure: Abutments and piers that provide the structure supporting the footbridge.

superstructure: The upper part of the footbridge structure comprising the deck, the structure supporting the deck and safety railing.

Path Surfacing

causey path: A path laid across deep peat.

fines: Aggregates that are laid on the top of a path to form a solid walkway.

stone pitching: A durable technique for laying paths in natural stone.

INDEX

abutment 158
access gate 51–61
access, history of 10–14
aggregates 134, 138, 142,
    145, 154
airlift planning 26–27
airlift safety 27–28
Areas of Outstanding
    Natural Beauty 12–13
artificial seeding 136
auto latch 62
axe 23

bar strainer 17
baseboard 70–71
baskets (for gabions)
    80–82
batter 76
batter frame 76, 77
billhook 23
bowsaw 23
bridle gate 62–64
bridle latch 63–64
bridleways 8, 138–154
brush cutter 19–20
brushing hook 23
Byeway Open to All Traffic
    (BOAT) 9
byeways 9

cabin hook 58
cages (for gabions) 81–82
cat scan 18, 19
causey paths 128–132
chain strainer 17
chainsaw 19
chisel 21–22
clamp 23
clapper bridge 131–132

clapper post 48, 62–63
clinometer 88
coir matting 83
compass 30–31, 37–40
contour lines 35–37
coping stone 60, 75, 76,
    122–124
corners in steps 97–99
Countryside and Rights of
    Way Act 2000 11–14
courses (of walling) 75, 79,
    82
cross-fall 111
crowbar 17, 18
culvert 148–152
curved steps 97–99

disabled access 41
drainage 131, 133, 134,
    138, 147–152
dry stone wall 72, 75–79
duckboard bridge 160

earth wall revetment
    72–74
electrical tools 20–21
end stones 78
erosion 65, 80, 125–137,
    153

fabric membrane 144
face-stones 76, 78–79
fencing 118
fencing maul 17, 66
fencing strainers 17
fetilizer 137
fines 141, 146
fingerpost 167–170
flagstone bridge 132

footbridge 155–166
Footpath Diversion Order
    155
footpaths 8, 138–154
foundation trench 106,
    107, 112, 140, 146
fuel safety 28

gabions 80–83
gate stoop 45–46, 52, 62
geotextile membrane
    141–145
green lanes 9
grid references and
    squares 33–35

hacksaw 22
hand repair of paths 133
hand saw 22
hand tools 17–23
handrails 99–104,
    163–164
Health and Safety
    Executive (HSE) 16
hearting stones 76, 82
helicopters 24–28
hinges 46–47, 53–55
hoggin 142, 143

kissing gate 41–50

landings 105–115
landscaping gabions
    82–83
large inclines 90–97
laying boarding 68–72
Least Restrictive Option
    (LRO) 41
Leptospyrosis 23

limestone 40–141, 146
line-level 76
Local Highways Authority
  7–8
lopper 23

machine repair of paths
  133
maps 8–9, 30, 32–40
materials 28–29, 42,
  65–66, 74, 85–87,
  99–100, 105, 116, 134,
  138, 140, 156–157
mattock 17
monkey strainer 17
nailing up steps 89, 94

National Trails 9–10
natural stone revetments
  75–79
netting 100, 103–104

path cross-section 139
peat 128–132, 142
pick 17
plant equipment 20
plasticizer 105
platform 89–90, 91, 96
post slammer 18
post-and-rail fence 61
posthole 44–45, 52, 92,
  101–102
power lines (underground)
  18, 19
preparing a path for boarding 66–68
public right of way 7–8, 10,
  155
punner 17

ranging pole 155
repairing an uphill section
  of path 72–74
restoration problems
  135–136
revegetation 134–137
revetment boarding 65–74,
  98–99, 139
riser 85–86, 88–89, 91–95,
  97–98
risk assessment 15–16
Road Used as a Public
  Path (RUPP) 9
rows of steps 111–112
runner 60, 78

safe area 18
safety 15–23, 27–28
safety glasses/goggles 66
screwdriver 22
scythe 23
shoveholer 51
shovel 17, 18
sickle 23
sledge hammer 17
sleeper-style bridge
  156–166
soil stabilization 137
spade 17, 18
spring 56–58
squeeze stile 124
stakes 70–71, 85–87,
  92–94, 98, 101–102
step-over drainage 131
steps 105, 112–115
stiles 116–124
stob 85
stock proofing 100, 103,
  116, 124

stock wire 102–104
stone flag surfacing
  129–132, 151
stone pitching 127–128,
  138, 153–154
stone stiles 119–124
stone toe 82
surfacing a path 74

tamper 17, 18
through stone 60, 78
tools 17–23, 28–29, 66,
  87, 101, 106, 116,
  143–144, 157
top stone 60
torsion bar 66
transplanting 136–137
treads 119–124

universal fencing tool 17

vehicular use 139,
  140–141, 155
vibrating plate 144–146

wall foundation 77–78
walling 59–61, 74, 75–79,
  106–107
walling hammer 76
way mark 167–170
Weil's Disease 23
wet-stone walling 75
windlass 67, 71–72
wooden revetment 73
wooden steps 84–104
wooden stiles 116–118